THE
MORAL
IMPERATIVE

Vincent Ryan Ruggiero

The
Moral
Imperative

AN INTRODUCTION TO ETHICAL JUDGMENT, WITH CONTEMPORARY ISSUES FOR ANALYSIS

Alfred Publishing Co., Inc.

Library of Congress Catalog Card Number: 73-78659

I.S.B.N.: 088284-007-X

To

Vincent V. Ruggiero, my father,
the late Filomena Ruggiero, my grandmother,
Francis and Michael Ruggiero, my uncles,
and Edith and Bernhard Theisselmann, my "extra parents,"
whose quiet lessons and example first introduced
me to the subject of this book.

Contents

THE SAME MORAL ISSUES that men and women have grappled with throughout history have grown ever more difficult in a society whose structures and forms are changing. And the impressive advances of science and technology have created a host of new issues.

Yet precisely at this time, when we most need a firm intellectual foundation to guide our judgment, we are confused by countless challenges to old and familiar faiths and standards.

The outlines of our very humanity are blurred by conflicting theories.

This, then, is the moral imperative of our time—to break the bonds of indecision, move beyond fad and foolishness, and address the dilemmas of modern living, sensitively and sensibly, with regard for their complexity.

Acknowledgments

I AM GRATEFUL TO all who had a part in the making of this book. Special thanks go to Herbert Sorgen, Librarian of Delhi College, for his assistance in research; to my students, for their helpful criticism; to Miss Mildred Beckwith, for preparing the manuscript; to Professor Gaston Pelletier, for suggesting the title; and to the executive and editorial staff of Alfred Publishing Company, for humanizing the publishing process.

Introduction

THIS BOOK is designed to achieve what Alfred North Whitehead prescribed for all education: an emphasis on principles rather than details.

It is intended to be a compromise between rigor and relevance: presenting standards of inquiry and judgment, but avoiding the dullness and heaviness of reading material that is too often associated with such standards; relating to important present concerns, but without pandering to intellectual fashion.

It is also intended to be clear and readable enough to capture some of the drama, excitement, and immediacy of the ethical issues it discusses, so that reading it will be a pleasure instead of a punishment—the kind of book that someone not enrolled in a college course might *choose* to read.

Most important, it is intended to be usable in a number of courses. Moral judgment is one of the distinguishing potentials of man. It should be as natural to a person as breathing. Therefore, it doesn't belong only in the seldom-traveled regions of the curriculum, in elective courses frequented by handfuls of students. It belongs in the center. Accordingly, the book is designed to fit a variety of courses in addition to the ethics course: the composition or speech course, the social science course, the interdisciplinary course; any course, in fact, which aims at developing sound moral judgment in the student.

The design of the book reflects these intentions. The chapters are brief. There are no complicated readings. (Where appropriate, the instructor can supplement the book with a collection of readings.) There are numerous cases in the chapters to illustrate the principles and approaches, and timely, thought-provoking cases for analysis and discussion.

In short, this is a book which will not daunt, impress, or humble those who read it; nor even, as current jargon would have it, "expose" them to the subject of ethics. But it may interest them, arouse their enthusiasm, and encourage them to *do* ethical judgment instead of witnessing it done. Moral inquiry is, after all, too important to every individual to be merely a spectator sport.

Why do we need ethics? We have laws to protect people's rights. We have religious beliefs to guide their actions. If the laws are enforced and the beliefs followed, what need have we of further rules?

A CAR SPEEDS THROUGH a red light at a crowded intersection; a squad car begins pursuit, light flashing and siren screaming. Two men are fighting in a bar; one pulls a knife, stabs the other, and runs out; the proprietor calls the police, who seek out the assailant. A store owner arrives at his place of business one morning and finds it has been burglarized; he reports the burglary, and detectives begin searching for clues to the burglar's identity.

Such events are unfortunately common. And there is nothing strange or unusual about the behavior of the police in response to them. In each case a law has been broken, and the police are doing their job—investigating the details of the case and apprehending suspects.

If asked where the laws came from, we'd have little difficulty answering. They are made by legislators, "lawmakers," at various levels of government: local, state, national. But if we were asked what the legislators based those laws on, we might have more difficulty answering. Why did they prohibit speeding through red lights, stabbing others, breaking into others' places of business and taking their property? The answer we would undoubtedly be driven to, after experiencing the frustration of groping for a more definitive response, is "Because those actions were wrong!"

With such cases, that answer would usually satisfy. Not so in all cases, however. Why can't a wage-earner choose not to file an income tax return or use a different tax schedule from the one provided on the government form? Why can't a person grow marijuana in his backyard or smoke it in the privacy of his own home? To say we can't perform these actions because they are wrong is not enough. For the question that leaps forth from that response is "But *why* are they wrong?" And to answer it we must do something more than invoke the laws themselves. We have to look to the moral perspective that underlies them.

If the laws themselves were a trustworthy measure of the rightness of actions, then there could not be a bad law. Every law would of necessity be just. Yet we know that some laws are unjust despite the good intentions of lawmakers. That is, they punish behavior that does not deserve punishment. The 18th amendment to the U.S. Constitution made Prohibition the law of the land . . . until the 21st amendment repealed it in the name of justice. Members of the Amish religious sect, whose way of life called for less formal schooling than the law prescribed, were judged criminals for withdrawing their children from school . . . until the U.S. Supreme Court declared the application of the law to them unjust.

Ethics Precedes Law

Laws are, in large part, a reflection of a country's conclusions about right and wrong. Those conclusions are separate from the law and precede it. They are not fixed and immutable, but alive and growing, changing as imperceptibly as our culture changes, responding to its challenges. They provide us all, including legislators and jurists, with a perspective from which to evaluate and classify actions, approving some, disapproving others.

The study that develops our perspective of right and wrong is the study of ethics. Ethics concerns moral situations, that is, *those situations in which there is a choice of behavior involving human values*, those qualities which are regarded as good and desirable. Thus, whether we watch TV at a friend's house or at our own is not a moral issue. But whether we watch TV at his house without his knowledge and approval is. Similarly, filling out an application

6

for a job is a morally neutral act. But deciding whether to tell the truth on the form is a moral decision. An ethicist is one who observes the choices people make in various moral situations and draws conclusions about them. An ethical system is a set of coherent conclusions forming an overall outlook about a range of moral situations.

Unlike a legal system, which is a set of do's and don't's designed to protect people's rights and the public order and to dispense justice in disputes among citizens, an ethical system produces no body of rules and regulations. Ethicists are not lawmakers. They are neither elected nor appointed. Their only authority is the force of reasonableness in their judgments. Their words, unlike those of law, do not prescribe what must or must not be done. They merely offer suggestions about behavior. If someone violates his own or his society's moral code, no ethics enforcement agency will try to apprehend him—though if his action also violates a law, a law enforcement agency may do so.

Law enforcement, of course, extends beyond apprehension of alleged criminals. It includes the formal trial and judgment of guilt or innocence, and there are degrees of guilt. A person who carries out a carefully planned murder is charged with a more serious crime than a person who strikes and kills another in spontaneous, blind rage. In fact, if the second man is judged to have been temporarily insane, he may go entirely unpunished.

This idea of varying degrees of responsibility for one's actions is applied in ethics, too. And though there are no courts of ethics as there are courts of law, and no formal pronouncements of guilt or innocence in actual cases, the ethicist nevertheless is interested in the question, "Under what circumstances is a person to be counted culpable?" (Here, as in the case of *lawmaking*, the thoughts of ethicists provide a foundation for legal judgments.)

Religious Belief No Substitute

So much for the relation of ethics and law. But what of the relation between ethics and religious belief? Isn't right and wrong a religious matter? And shouldn't it therefore be decided in a religious context? The answer depends on several considerations. First, it depends on what we mean by a "religious matter." If we mean morality is a spiritual affair in the sense that it reflects the quality of one's character, then yes. But if we mean by religious matter, "subject to a particular institutional church and its doctrine," the answer is no. For no one religion can claim jurisdiction over the consideration of right and wrong. That is a human matter, a subject of human interest independent of any religious belief.

It is, of course, as acceptable as it is common for a church to believe that its moral values are better than those of others. But if any church wants to persuade others of such a belief, it must seek some common ground, some mutually shared approach to ethical issues. And if it wishes to extend its dialogue to those with very different religious beliefs or no religious belief, then it must adopt its criteria of judgment very carefully.

It is not very helpful, for example, to judge actions by the criterion of whether they "please or offend God." For the question that naturally arises is "How do you know they do?" And the two most common answers serve more to close off ethical inquiry than to promote it. One is, "Because the Bible says so." The other is, "This is my belief." To pursue the matter further, we are placed in the position of having to challenge the Bible or to invade the very private domain of the other person's belief and challenge something precious to him.

Both answers, in addition, are based on erroneous notions. Saying "the Bible says so" suggests that the Bible is a simple book that doesn't admit of more than a single interpretation. Yet biblical scholarship clearly demonstrates that it is highly complex and permits numerous interpretations. (If it were not so, then biblical study would not be the demanding and rewarding pursuit it is.) Saying "this is my belief" implies that no aspect of a person's belief can be shallow or mistaken, that in matters religious there is no room for growth and development. The lives of the saints and holy men of the world's religions disprove any such notion.

There are some ethical questions which cannot be adequately answered by reference to our religious beliefs alone. Take, for example, the case of a person pondering this question: "Since I no longer accept some of the major teachings of the church I was raised in, is it morally right for me to remain a member? What ought I to do?" The question is by no means an easy one, though it may appear so. But whatever approach he might use in answering it, the teachings of his religion would hardly be the definitive measure. For they are an integral part of the question. Using them would be equivalent to affirming them.

In other cases, religious beliefs may speak very directly but too narrowly. Consider this case. A middle-aged grade school teacher is found to belong to a mate-swapping club. The school board decides that her behavior, though clearly a private matter, is likely to be a source of scandal to the community. Therefore, they summarily dismiss her. The question under consideration is, was the board's decision ethically justifiable? To answer it fairly, we should approach it openmindedly. Yet if our religious belief includes strong prohibitions against adultery and scandal, but virtually none against job discrimination because of life style, we might approach the question with our minds made up. We might be unable even to consider the possibility that the teacher was wronged.

Happily, most religious thinkers recognize the error of judging moral issues merely by religious belief. They realize the importance of discussing them in a way that is meaningful and appealing to all men of good will and honest concern, a way that not only expresses their understanding of human behavior, but tests it and helps it to expand. For this reason, they distinguish carefully between religious belief and religious ethics. Religious ethics is the examination of moral situations from a particular religious perspective. In it, the religious doctrine is not a substitute for inquiry. It is a starting point, a guide to inquiry and to organizing the findings of inquiry.

Some Guidelines to Inquiry

In the case of the mate-swapping grade school teacher, we noted how religious belief can lead to prejudging the case. This problem is not, of course, limited to believers. An unbeliever who felt strongly that adultery is morally acceptable but job discrimination because of life style is reprehensible might approach the issue with his mind made up too. The possibility that the board acted correctly might be inconceivable to him.

Few people are completely free from the inclination to prejudgment in at least some issues. One person may have his answer ready for any question concerning war. Another may for questions concerning private property. Still others may for issues involving alcohol or drugs. And many will for cases of sexual morality. The reasons for prejudging will vary—from traumatic experience to personal preference to simple opinion. The underlying attitudes may range from distrust of all regulations, all laws, even all *thoughts,* to an uncritical endorsement of all traditions. But in each case the effect is the same: to avoid thinking about the particular case at all, and merely call forth a prefabricated, all-purpose answer.

The alternative to the closed mind is not the empty mind, however. Even if we wished to set aside completely all our prior conclusions about human behavior and right and wrong, we couldn't do so. The mind can't be manhandled that way. Nor should it be. We can expect, then, that a flood of impressions and reactions will rush in upon our thoughts when we consider a moral issue. It is not the fact of that flood that matters, nor its force. It is what we do to avoid having our judgment swept away by it. Here are some suggestions:

1 *Observe those first impressions. Note them carefully.* Knowing the way our thinking inclines is the first step toward balancing it.

2 *Don't express first impressions in discussion or writing.* It's natural to want to defend our position, especially if it's challenged by someone else. To abandon it is to lose face. By not stating it or even writing it down until we're sure of it, we can remain flexible.

3 *Consider several different positions and the arguments that could be used to support them.* The position that directly opposes our first impression is often the most helpful one to consider. If our impression is wrong, this will help us find out. If it was not, then we can return to it with confidence and present it more effectively for having considered the alternatives to it.

INQUIRIES

1 Wiretapping is legal with court authorization. Is it also morally right? Is wiretapping ever morally right without court authorization? Consider these cases. (a) the police receive a tip that someone is engaged in smuggling marijuana into the United States from Mexico; (b) the FBI uncovers a plot to assassinate top government officials and take over the government; (c) a suspicious husband suspects his wife of having an affair with someone.

2 A village bordering on the ocean places restrictions on the use of its beaches. Residents of the village are issued beach passes for themselves and their guests. All others are barred. Is such a restriction a moral issue? That is, is it debatable in terms of right and wrong? Explain.

3 There is no legal obligation for an eligible voter to vote in an election in this country. Is the decision to vote or not to vote a moral decision? Explain.

4 As a condition for the continuation of federal aid, the federal government requires colleges to file a plan for achieving racial and ethnic balance in their professional staffs. This has the effect of giving a black or Puerto Rican applicant a clear advantage over a white applicant, even though the white applicant may be better qualified for the position. Is such a requirement ethically justifiable? Explain.

5 Certain people have spoken out against the government's foreign and domestic policies. They have broken no laws. Their protests have been fully within the guarantees of free speech. Yet the FBI is directed to investigate each thoroughly. They conduct background studies, including interviews with relatives, friends, and acquaintances. Are these investigations ethically justifiable? Explain.

6 A married couple, both addicted to drugs, are unable to care for their infant daughter. She is taken from them by court order and placed in a foster

home. The years pass. She comes to regard her foster parents as her real parents. They love her as they would their own daughter. Then, when she is nine years old, her natural parents, rehabilitated from drugs, initiate court action to regain the child. The case is decided in their favor. The child is returned to them, against her will. Does ethics support the law in this case? Discuss.

7 A sociology professor spots a magazine article that will fit in well with the textbook chapter he has assigned his students. However, copyright law forbids his making copies of it without obtaining the publisher's or author's permission (usually given for a small fee). Since he cannot use college funds for this purpose, and since there isn't sufficient time to go through the process of obtaining permission, he decides to break the law and make the copies. Does he act rightly? Explain.

8 Federal agents, acting on a tip that $4 million in profits from the sale of heroin was hidden in a roofing contractor's home, obtained a search warrant, entered his home, and proceeded to tear it apart. Walls were torn down, furniture ripped apart, the siding and patio tiles loosened, trenches were dug in his yard, the toilet bowl was smashed. The "work" went on for almost 24 hours, and caused an estimated $50,000 damage. The owner, who is married to the sister of a convicted narcotics dealer, but has no criminal record himself, sued for damages. But the problem was that the law was vague on the point. One law professor stated that there was virtually no legal precedent for such a suit. Nor was it clear who should be held responsible. The federal government? The federal agents? Their supervisor? (After the incident, the supervisor said he still believed the men conducted a "reasonable search.")[1] Frame your own answer to these questions from an ethical standpoint.

9 In recent years a number of cemeteries around the U.S. have opened their gates to a variety of types of leisure activities: for example, cycling, jogging, fishing, nature hiking, and even team sports.[2] Is the opening of cemeteries to these activities a moral issue? If so, what are some of the considerations that make it so?

Religion

Business & Finance

MONTERREY STOCK EXCHANGE

28

The New Yor...
Stock Exchange

Business & Finance

2

How do we account for the fact that an action that is praised in one culture may be condemned in another? Doesn't this suggest that all moral values are relative to the culture they are found in?

IT IS A FACT that cultures differ in their ideas about right and wrong. And the differences are not always slight. In more than a few instances, one culture's sin is another's virtue. For example, the conception of marriage that we are most familiar with—one wife and one husband joined for life—is not universal. In some cultures serial monogamy is not merely tolerated (as it is beginning to be in the United States), but actually regarded as neutral or even good. And in Siberia, where Women's Liberation would appear to be neglected, "a Koryak woman . . . would find it hard to understand how a woman could be so selfish and so undesirous of female companionship in the home as to wish to restrict her husband to one mate."[1]

Sex before marriage has been generally viewed as immoral in the West. Yet in some island cultures, it is not only not frowned upon, but positively encouraged.

A New Jerseyite who offers his wife to his overnight guest is a pervert. Yet an Eskimo who does exactly the same thing is a thoughtful host. Homosexuals are hounded and tormented as immoral deviants in some cultures; in others they are accepted without reservation.

Such differences are not limited to sexual morality. It is considered a person's moral obligation in some cultures to assist a blood relative in any enterprise, even stealing from others. Certain tribes of head-hunters may raid neighboring villages and return with the villagers' heads for no greater reason than that their "supply" of names is used up and for a new name to be claimed, one must possess the head it belonged to.[2] Yet in the recently discovered Tasaday tribe of the Philippines, violence is apparently unknown.

It is commonly thought that at least one action—the taking of life—would be unanimously condemned by people of all cultures. Here is what Ruth Benedict has to say about that idea in her classic study, *Patterns of Culture:*

> On the contrary, in a matter of homicide, it may be held that one is blameless if diplomatic relations have been severed between neighbouring countries, or that one kills by custom his first two children, or that a husband has right of life and death over his wife, or that it is the duty of the child to kill his parents before they are old. It may be that those are killed who steal a fowl, or who cut their upper teeth first, or who are born on a Wednesday. Among some peoples a person suffers torments at having caused an accidental death; among others it is a matter of no consequence. Suicide also may be a light matter, the recourse of anyone who has suffered some slight rebuff, an act that occurs constantly in a tribe. It may be the highest and noblest act a wise man can perform. The very tale of it, on the other hand, may be a matter for incredulous mirth, and the act itself impossible to conceive as a human possibility. Or it may be a crime punishable by law, or regarded as a sin against the gods.[3]

Miss Benedict details in that volume the customs, values, and beliefs of three cultures. One of them is that of several groups of Indians of the northwest coast of America, mainly the Kwakiutl of Vancouver Island. Their culture lasted until the end of the nineteenth century. Among these tribes it was accepted practice to murder a person to acquire the rights to his name, his special dances, his personal crests and symbols. Stranger still was their way of dealing with the sadness of mourning the death of a loved one. They merely found someone of equal rank in a neighboring tribe, announced their intention of killing him, and then proceeded to do so. Thus they bested fate and the pain of sorrow by not reacting passively, but by striking back.[4]

The most interesting of the cultures described by Miss Benedict, however, is surely that of Dobu Island off the coast of New Guinea. The Dobuans' entire life is spent in the most vicious competition. The rule of virtually every social enterprise is *cheat your neighbor.* The good man, the respected man, is the one who has succeeded in foxing his opponent. The Dobuan who wishes to injure someone, unlike the Northwest Coastal Indian, does not announce his plan, but pretends affection, and does his treachery in secret or by surprise. The sorcery which they practice on one another is, in their view, made more potent by closeness to the victim.

One of the most enviable accomplishments of Dobuan life is the successful practice of *wabuwabu*. By it a person victimizes another. He may promise to deliver in trade the same valuable possession to several traders, or break an engagement for marriage after obtaining the usual property settlement from the father of the betrothed. "It is taken for granted," Miss Benedict notes, "that the Dobuan has thieved, killed children and his close associates by sorcery, cheated whenever he dared."[5]

Interpreting Cultural Differences

What are we to make of such differences among cultures? What conclusions are we to draw? The principle that covers such cases is the principle of cultural relativity. It means that the ingredients of a culture do not depend on any absolutes outside that culture and above all cultures, but that they vary according to the background and development and natural habitat of the particular culture. By "ingredients," we mean all important matters of the culture's life: social customs, religious rituals, mythology, attitudes toward nature and other peoples.

In the largest sense this principle of cultural relativity is too obvious to be disputed. And yet it is controversial because it has been subject to divergent interpretations. What is the basis of the controversy? Not so much the principle itself, as the conclusions that some leap to from the principle. The most common conclusion is that "If there is no observable control transcending all cultures, no eternal book of rules, then right and wrong are a matter of opinion and it doesn't matter what we do: *anything goes!"*

This conclusion does not, however, necessarily follow from the principle. Some authorities, in fact, declare that this conclusion is decidedly what cultural relativity does *not* mean. "The principle of cultural relativity," Clyde Kluckhohn writes, "does not mean that because the members of some savage tribe are allowed to behave in a certain way that this fact gives intellectual warrant for such behavior in all groups. Cultural relativity means, on the contrary, that the appropriateness of any positive or negative custom must be evaluated with regard to how this habit fits with other group habits."[6]

In their studies of other cultures, modern anthropologists have found that it is all too easy to misinterpret people's behavior. What seems to be so may not really be so. Just as it is natural for us to read the behavior of others in terms of our own standards, so it is natural to view actions in other cultures from the codes of our culture. What seems fair to us we assume is fair to them; and when we see an action we regard as treacherous, we likewise assume that they have violated their code. Yet a deeper understanding of their code may reveal that they have not only not been violating it, but in fact observing it.

The only way to penetrate the deception of appearance is to study the cultural context in which the action occurs, determining the circumstances of time, place, and condition surrounding it and, most important, learning the reasoning that underlies it and the moral value it reflects.

Kluckhohn cites an example from World War II. The behavior of Japanese captives confounded American military men. Within the same week, on occasion, the same Japanese who had demonstrated fanatical allegiance to their Emperor, to the point of risking their lives in suicide missions, would when captured write propaganda for the Americans, reveal information about Japanese bases, and even fly reconnaisance missions against their own people. To many American servicemen such behavior must have seemed despicably cowardly and positively immoral. Yet to anthropologists familiar with the Japanese ethical system, Kluckhohn notes, the behavior was not mysterious at all. For Japanese morality was *situational*. In the situation where they were fighting in the service of the Emperor, their morality bid them serve him unquestioningly. But in the situation of capture, that same morality bid them transfer their allegiance to the new authority, their captors.[7]

The very strangeness of ways of thinking and acting that are foreign to us can lead us to overemphasize the differences among cultures. New and familiar things always have a certain dramatic impact. And so the exciting details of anthropological studies make it tempting to reason that, if the morality of actions is so widely different, then the underlying values the actions are based on must also be radically different. In some cases they indeed are. According to the Dobuan's view of life, as we have seen, "virtue consists in selecting a victim upon whom he can vent the malignancy he attributes alike to human society and to the powers of nature."[8]

The Similarity of Values

But the Dobuan's culture is in this respect quite atypical. In other cultures the differences in values are more apparent than real. Sometimes the difference in behavior is attributable to a *different way of viewing the same value*, as in the case of the Japanese prisoners of war. At other times it is attributable to *the observance of a religious belief or taboo*, as in the case of the Indian's refusal to kill a sacred cow, even to provide food for starving people. At still other times it reflects *the belief that some other, higher value takes precedence*. The Northwest Coastal Indian's practice of taking a life to balance the death of a loved one is an example. The reason for his action is not that he lacks a sense of fairness to his victim, but that heroic retaliation against life's tragedies is a prior obligation.

Even in cases where none of the above explanations applies, a value may, because of a people's behavior, appear absent but actually be present. In such cases, *the value is simply not considered applicable to the victims*. Consider two cases discussed earlier in the chapter: the man who helped his relative steal and the headhunters who replenished their supply of names. Surely they seemed to be acting without a sense of justice or fairness. Yet both were in fact acting on the idea that *outsiders*, those alien to family or tribe, are "beyond the pale of moral consideration."[9] Justice and fairness are seen as not covering them. They are not persons; hence they have no rights. (If such reasoning seems bizarre, remember that many American slaveowners had similar attitudes toward their slaves, and that the domestic and foreign policies of "civilized" countries do not always, even to this day, coincide.)

The conclusion that even these few cases suggest is that the rules of behavior may vary greatly from culture to culture, but that the underlying values are usually similar, often remarkably so. There is justice and courage, respect for one's relatives and tribesmen, subordination of individual whim to custom or the judgments of tribal sages. And if it is a mistake to deny the differences in human values, such as the aberrant Dobuan culture represents, then surely it is an even greater mistake to deny the similarities.

INQUIRIES

In each of the following cases, the behavior illustrated seems to suggest that the people's values differ significantly from our own. Consider the possibility that, beneath appearances, the values are similar. Develop a plausible explanation for the difference in behavior.

1 In one culture, the elderly and those with severe handicaps are put to death. It would appear this culture does not recognize human dignity as a value.

2 In another culture this habit is observed: a man will ask his relative to do a task that requires days of labor and, when it is completed, never even thank him. On the other hand, if a stranger renders anyone the slightest service, he is lavishly rewarded. It would appear that a sense of fairness is lacking in this culture.

3 A common practice of a tribe living in a remote jungle area is to shun the sick. The moment a member of the tribe becomes seriously ill, he ceases to exist in the tribe's view. He must leave the village and care for himself. If he recovers, however, he is restored to tribal membership. Apparently, the tribe lacks compassion for the afflicted.

4   A group of young boys are gathered together. Several men approach them, brandishing sticks and whips. They beat the boys viciously. The other male members of the tribe sit by and watch, laughing and obviously enjoying the event. It would seem that the men of this culture are sadistic, deriving pleasure from seeing others in pain.

5   Whenever a hunter in a certain culture is asked how his day's hunting went, he says "very well" and goes on to declare that his relatives and friends and ancestors will be pleased with him. He says this whether he returns heavily laden or emptyhanded. It appears that truth-telling has no value in this culture.

6   One woman finds another eating a piece of wild fruit. She calls to her neighbors and they stone the offender to death. Since the punishment does not fit the crime, it would appear that this culture lacks a sense of proportion and fails to recognize the value of human life.

7   In an island culture, the men are seen returning from a fishing expedition. One man runs his canoe happily up on the beach. The villagers cheer him. Then a second canoe arrives. The second fisherman leaps out, runs to the first man, seizes his basket of fish and throws it into the sea. He goes unpunished. The tribe seems to tolerate stealing.

3

But doesn't the fact of such great differences in basic ethical judgments (if not in underlying values) among cultures caution us against claiming that any culture is better than others? And isn't it a mark of ignorance to pass judgment on the morality of those who disagree with us?

THE PHRASING chosen for the above questions is deliberate. It matches the phrasing commonly used in expressing this widespread viewpoint. The problem with it, however, is that it is ambiguous in two ways. What does "better than" mean? And precisely what kind of "judgment" is referred to?

"Better than" is obviously a term of comparison. It has many variations: people speak of cultures being "higher than" others, or "surpassing" them. But whenever someone makes this kind of comparison—"The Egyptian culture was better than the Roman" or "Our culture has surpassed all others"—the sensitive person cringes. Rightly so. For such statements have one of two implications. The first is that the "higher" culture has outdistanced the other in every particular of language, custom, behavior, learning, artistic achievement, and material accomplishment. Such a performance may be theoretically possible, but it is quite improbable. Proclaiming it casually, without documentation, invites disbelief. The other possible implication is that one culture has bested the other in some overall tally in which virtues are added and vices subtracted. And that is ludicrous.

Thus, "better than" comparisons are rightly seen as presumptuous. And it is understandable that because of them many are led to reject all comparisons of cultures, to suspend all evaluation. That is a mistake. What is wrong with "better than" comparisons is not that they dare to make value judgments about cultures, but that they do so in a loose, sweeping manner, and without specifying exactly what is being judged.

Reasonable value judgments about other cultures are quite possible. Consider, for example, these two modest judgments: "Culture A has achieved a less violent attitude toward its neighbors than culture B." "In sharp contrast to culture C, culture D practices admirable tolerance of homosexuals." We might argue, I suppose, that peaceableness is not an unmixed blessing in a people, or that treatment should precede tolerance of homosexuals. And after learning the facts that preceded the judgments, we might disagree with the judgments. Nevertheless, we would not consider such judgments to be necessarily foolish or improper.

There is nothing wrong in the idea that each culture must honor its own perspective on life and must not be condemned for any actions, however heinous, that derive from that perspective. And it is natural enough if that idea, fanned by a sense of democracy, leads to this kind of reasoning: "Well, we disapprove of headhunting, but then the Wugabuga tribe approves of it, so it's wrong for us but right for them."

Such thinking seems unassailable. It demonstrates charity, humility, a live-and-let-live generosity. Unfortunately, it sits on the brink of absurdity. We are safe only so long as we heed the counsel of intellectual honesty and good sense, which says in response: "Right for them but wrong for us? No, that's nonsense. Despite the fact that our cultures differ, despite the fact that the Wugabuga's headhunting is perfectly understandable given their history, geography, and world-view, headhunting is not justifiable. It is an invasion of the basic rights of the victims. Admittedly, the Wugabuga do not acknowledge those rights. But they *should*. And given further development and increased contact with other peoples, they surely will recognize the need to do so."

The distinction between *understanding* and *justification* is a crucial one. As human beings, imperfect in our grasp of reality, necessarily groping toward our answers, we must constantly reach out to others and strive to understand their views. To be closed to others' views and the reasoning that leads to them, to judge these matters in ignorance, or in the twilight of fragmentary knowledge, is to stunt our growth as human beings. Yet explanation is not justification. The ancient Spartans had a very logical reason for whipping young boys viciously. It was a ritual that marked their introduction into manhood and symbolized the physical toughness required of the citizens of a warrior-state. But that reason doesn't make the action right.

Similarly, we can thoroughly understand the thinking of slavetraders without approving their occupation. And we can gain deep psychological insights into the Nazi persecution of the Jews—indeed, insights that the Nazis themselves could not grasp—and yet condemn their program of extermination as utterly wrong.

Judgment Is Unavoidable

The behavior of other cultures in certain situations sheds light on our behavior in similar situations. For example, in ancient Persia and Egypt criminals were not only used in medical experiments; they were treated more like laboratory animals than human beings. In the eighteenth century, the Princess of Wales had six condemned criminals and six poor children vaccinated against smallpox to determine whether the vaccine would be safe for her children. Had they died (in her view, before any real harm was done), she would have decided not to vaccinate her children. Early in this century at Harvard a professor of medicine infected some criminals with plague, allegedly without their consent, as an experiment.[1]

Did the Harvard professor act ethically? Whatever our answer, we probably have no qualms about answering. But dare we evaluate a case in eighteenth-century England? And should we presume to pass judgment on the case in ancient Persia and Egypt? *We cannot help but do so.* For in all three cases we are dealing with essentially the same situation. And though, since circumstances alter cases, we could judge each differently, any judgment we made of one would have implications for the others.

All this is not to say that judgments of other cultures should be made perfunctorily. On the contrary, they should be made very carefully and tentatively. The attitude that should permeate all our inquiry into other cultures is that every culture is human and therefore no culture (including our own) is perfect, that every culture has its areas of moral sensitivity and insensitivity. Everyone has his portion of wisdom and of ignorance. So each has much to learn from the others.

Issues in Our Culture

The most important focus of the chapters that follow, however, will not be the comparison of moral standards among the various cultures. It will be the analysis and judgment of moral issues in our culture and in our time. The familiarity of the social context will, in most cases, spare us the effort of learning new and unfamiliar social contexts. But it will pose the problem of dealing forcefully and honestly with contemporary issues. In some ways that problem is more difficult.

If we are alienated from our culture and reject its moral perspective, we will be inclined to overlook its virtues. And if, as is more likely, we accept its perspective, consciously or unconsciously, we will be inclined to overlook its shortcomings. In addition, when we share our culture's perspective, one crippling assumption is liable to run through all our evaluations: that its view is right because it's the latest. This oversimplifies reality. Just as it is possible for a culture to evolve its ethical sense to a high degree, and achieve profound moral insights, so too (alas) it is possible to slip backward, to become ethically insensitive, to replace insight with rationalization.

Another problem is the reluctance we naturally feel about judging contemporary moral issues. This often exceeds our reluctance to judge the morality of other cultures. The experimenting Harvard professor of fifty years ago, of course, like the slaveowner of earlier times, poses little problem. Both are removed from our day. But with our relatives and friends, our teachers and roommates in college, the writers and media "personalities" we revere, we feel obliged to forego moral judgment. The same democratic spirit we feel toward the Wugabuga tribe, we feel even more intensely toward our own tribe. "To each his own," we say. "Who am I to judge?"

The kinds of moral issues we must deal with today add to our tendency to respond this way. For the issues are controversial, perplexing, sometimes without precedent. The very mention of abortion triggers strong sentiments. The question of what weapons are legitimate in a war of defense is fraught with complexity. And the issues of genetic engineering and chemical stimulation of the brain pose new dilemmas.

Yet though the urge to say "It's wrong to judge" is understandable, it is just as mistaken a response within a culture as it is among cultures. For judging an action is not the same as judging the person who performs it. "Love me, love my idea" is not a reasonable demand; and mature people know better than to make it. We can disagree with the conclusions of others without straining mutual respect and friendship because, though courtesy is a civilized requirement for dealing with other people, it does not extend to ideas.

It is true, of course, that judgment of others' views involves not only the risk of error, but also the risk of offending others. But the alternative is to evade judgment when judgment is needed, and that is unworthy of thinking creatures; or to feign approval where we secretly disapprove, and that is deceitful.

INQUIRIES

1 As was mentioned in Chapter 2, the Eskimo's sense of hospitality requires him to offer his wife to an overnight guest. In our culture this is considered wrong. Is one view more justifiable than the other? Explain your reasoning carefully.

2 The case of the Japanese fliers detailed in Chapter 2 reveals a different view of allegiance to authority than we are accustomed to. If American fliers were captured by the Japanese we would have expected them to retain their loyalty to the United States rather than transfer it to their captors. Is one of these views more justifiable? Explain.

3 In some ancient cultures a young maiden was sacrificed each year to insure a good harvest. In others, when the king died, many servants were killed and buried with him so that his needs in the afterlife could be suitably attended. Such practices are understandable, given the beliefs of the people. Are they morally right? Why or why not?

4 In ancient Rome, Sparta, and China defective children and unwanted children were abandoned to die. Comment on the morality of this practice.

5 In some cultures a man who kills someone by accident must support the victim's family thereafter. In our culture, we expect life insurance and social security to cover the family's needs. If the one responsible for the accident is found to be legally blameless, he is customarily considered morally blameless, as well. Compare and evaluate these moral views.

6 Socialists regard as immoral the capitalistic idea of private property and personal wealth. They believe not only that the "haves" should share with the "have-nots," but that much of the property now privately owned should be publicly owned, that workers and citizens should enjoy the profits of business and industry, and that limits should be placed on the material wealth a person can accumulate. Is this idea more or less justifiable ethically than the capitalistic idea?

7 Review the Dobuan moral code and underlying view of life presented in Chapter 2. To what extent is it ethically justifiable?

4

Is the basis for deciding moral values within a culture the majority view? In other words, if the majority of the citizens of our country should decide that a particular action is right, would that very decision make the action right?

WE LIVE IN AN AGE when statistics confront us at every turn. From the moment we arise, we are bombarded by authoritative voices thrusting percentages at us. "Sixty-seven point two percent of the American public support the President's tax program." "Seven out of ten doctors recommend No-Ouch tablets." "My group had ninety percent less underarm odor." So it's no surprise that we often think that more is better, and if the majority agree that something is so, then it must be so.

But what, after all, is the "majority"? It is nothing more than fifty-one percent or more of the *individuals* in a group. And though the conversion of a bunch of individual views into a statistic can create the impression of authoritativeness and wisdom, those qualities do not always result. There is no magic in majorities.

If we were to examine some majority and compare their individual thinking on the particular issue, what would we find? First, we'd find that actual knowledge of the issue varied widely among the individuals. Some would be well informed about all details. Others would be completely uninformed, yet unaware of their ignorance. And between these extremes would be the largest group: partly informed and partly ignorant, in some ways perceptive but in others confused or mistaken.

Secondly, we'd find significant variations in the degree and quality of consideration given the facts. Some individuals would have read or listened to the views of authorities, sorted out irrelevancies, appraised each authority's position in light of available evidence, and weighed all possible interpretations of the facts. Others would have taken the ultimate shortcut and foregone all inquiry on the assumption that their intuition is infallible. A large middle group would have made some inquiry, but less than exhaustive and sometimes less than adequate.

Finally, we'd find wide differences in the quality of judgment of the issue. Some would have judged quite objectively, avoiding preconceived notions and prejudices, and being critical of all views, including those to which they are naturally disposed. Others would have been ruled completely by emotion, their judgment little more than a conditioned reflex. And most, again, would have achieved some middle position in which thought and "gut reaction" intermingle to produce more or less objective conclusions.

A Sample Situation

To see how all these differences might work in an actual moral issue, let's take the question "Is it wrong to kill enemy civilians in time of war?" and imagine we had asked it of a representative sampling of the general public and a slender majority had answered in the negative. What variations in knowledge, inquiry, and judgment would the statistical report cover? What actual lines of thought might have occurred to the individuals in the majority? Here are some probabilities.

Mr. A: "If they started the war, then the blame would be on them and they'd deserve no mercy. They'd all be responsible for their government's actions; so all of them, civilians and soldiers alike, would be regarded as enemies. If they get hurt, that's the breaks."

Mr. B: "I fought in Vietnam and, believe me, in that war you couldn't tell a friend from an enemy. I've seen children waving and shouting greetings as they approached with explosives attached to their backs. I've seen peasants who'd shoot you in the back or direct you into a mine field after you'd given them candy. It can't be wrong to kill civilians in war because it's necessary for survival."

Mrs. C: "No, it's not wrong if it helps to shorten the war. In World War II we saved more deaths and injuries to our boys and brought them home sooner by dropping atom bombs on two Japanese cities. Many civilians were in those cities. But our main intention was not to kill civilians; it was to end the war. Therefore the bombing was justified."

Ms. D: "It's a complex question. It really depends on the circumstances. The bombing of Dresden, Hiroshima, and Nagasaki during World War II were very wrong in my view. Those targets were selected *because* they were population centers and their destruction would demoralize the enemy. In other words, civilians were deliberately singled out for elimination. No goal, however worthy, justifies such slaughter. On the other hand, in a guerrilla war, the distinction between combatant and noncombatant is somewhat blurred. Soldiers disguise themselves as civilians. And civilians are enlisted, sometimes against their will, to perform military acts. In such a war I can conceive of situations where the killing of civilians is justified; say, where a soldier is in doubt whether the civilian approaching him is armed and must choose to shoot or jeopardize his own life. Is it wrong to kill civilians? I'd have to say no, not necessarily."

Perhaps none of these views is the best one possible. But the last one is much more penetrating than the others. It shows a greater grasp of important distinctions and a deeper, more balanced understanding of the moral dilemma the question involves in actual situations. Yet this position would be lumped together with others, including the utterly shallow and morally insensitive first one. In statistical computation, yes or no is everything. The depth or shallowness of the thought that supports it is ignored. (It is possible, of course, for statistical reports to include the full answers, but even when they are set up to provide for them, which is seldom, the need for brevity often forces their omission.)

The Majority Can Err

In short, the majority view is less than perfect. And to assume that it is necessarily enlightened is a serious mistake. For if 1 percent or 49 percent of the population can be shallow or prejudiced in their view of an issue, so can 51 or 99 percent. Corporate ignorance is as common as corporate wisdom.

At various times in history the majority have supported outrageous deeds. In some ancient societies the majority believed in and practiced murdering female babies, abandoning crippled infants to die, murdering young men and women as sacrifices to the gods or to serve a deceased monarch in the afterlife. The majority have supported religious wars, child labor, even child prostitution. In Hitler's Germany the majority gave at least silent assent to the persecution of the Jews. For centuries the standard treatment of the mentally ill, universally accepted, bordered on torture. And until recently in the southern United States racial intermarriage was not only morally condemned but legally prohibited.

If the majority view determined right and wrong, then slavery was not wrong when it was practiced in America. It was right as long as the majority accepted it and became wrong only when over 50 percent of the people rejected it. If the majority's moral perspective cannot err, then the religious persecutions that drove the early colonists to this continent were not wrong, were not vices at all, but virtues. Such a view, of course, is nonsense. Slavery and religious persecution would be no less immoral if every country in the world approved them. So there must be more to right and wrong than a showing of hands.

To be sure, the majority view may be the only one a democratic society can follow in its procedures of representative government. And even in lawmaking, the majority view will rightly exert considerable influence on legislators (though the true statesman will not hesitate to go against the majority when he judges it in their interest for him to do so). But even in these necessary nods to the majority, there is no guarantee of correctness. The future of the country hangs precariously on the hope that, in urgent matters, the counsel of the majority will be the counsel of wisdom.

Yet in ethical judgment, where there is a singular potential for emotional reaction, and even self-deception, it is especially important not to slavishly follow the majority view. We do well to remember that, just as we view certain practices of past centuries as morally indefensible, so later generations may judge some of our practices similarly. Every age has its blindness, and perhaps even its barbarism.

36

INQUIRIES

1 In 1971, after a military court found Lt. Calley guilty of the premeditated murder of 22 civilians in the Vietnam village of My Lai and sentenced him to dismissal from the army, forfeiture of pay and privileges, and life imprisonment, a national poll revealed that 79 percent of the American public disapproved of the verdict and punishment, presumably on moral grounds.[1] Were the verdict and punishment ethically justifiable? Explain your position.

2 Two years after the U.S. Supreme Court's famous school desegregation order, a national poll revealed that 80 percent of the citizens of southern states opposed school desegregation. The same poll disclosed that 76 percent disapproved the Interstate Commerce Commission's order banning train, bus, and waiting room segregation.[2] Are such desegregation orders ethically valid? Comment.

3 A national poll, published in 1972, disclosed that 56 percent of the American people believe that persons convicted of murder should be sentenced to death.[3] Is that majority right? Is capital punishment ethically justifiable?

4 At various times polls have indicated that a majority of Americans favor the outlawing of the Communist Party. Is it ethically valid in a democracy to outlaw any political party which citizens might in good conscience choose to support?

5 A 16-year-old girl visits a birth control clinic and asks to be put on the pill. Since she is a minor, the clinic doctor who writes the prescription for her notifies her parents of his action. Very possibly a majority of Americans would approve of his action. Is the action ethical?

6 Apparently many Americans, perhaps a majority, continue to believe that marijuana should not be legalized. In other words, they approve the law's prohibiting the use of a substance which has not been proved harmful. Is such a prohibition ethically justifiable? Why or why not?

5

If the majority view doesn't determine the rightness of an action, should each person decide on the basis of his own feelings, desires, preferences?

THE IDEA OF EVERYONE deciding moral issues on the basis of his own feelings, desires, or preferences enjoys some popularity today. "Everyone doing his own thing" seems a very reasonable and tolerant approach to morality. It has an understandable appeal to young people who are inclined to challenge their parents' moral code, and to those of all ages who are disenchanted with traditional views. It also harmonizes well with the prevailing concern with individuality. If each person is an individual, different from all others, then his morality, it would seem, like his fingerprints, should reflect his uniqueness.

Those who take this view emphasize making one's lifestyle and moral perspective reflect his own needs and wants rather than some prefabricated set of principles that "society" sanctions. They value subjective validity more highly than external norms.

The conclusion that follows from this reasoning is that no one person's view is preferable to another's. Each is good in its own way. One man's religious ritual may be the next man's cardinal sin. Thus if a man and a woman want to marry, that's fine. (The same for a man and a man, a woman and a woman.) But if a couple choose to live together without marrying, that's fine too. Indeed, if twenty-two want to live together in multiple liaison, that is also fine. No one other than the individuals themselves has any right to concern himself about it. Freedom is the byword, rules and restrictions the only heresies.

Now the first thing to note about this perspective on morality is that it is not very new. Two centuries ago Jean Jacques Rousseau wrote, "What I feel is right is right, what I feel is wrong is wrong." And his idea about the relationship of the individual to society underlies the modern perspective. The individual, in his view, is inherently good; it is society with its artificial constraints that corrupts him. All the current prompting to "rid ourselves of all inhibitions" and, in more colloquial form, "let it all hang out" have a kinship with Rousseau's thoughts.

There is no question, of course, that a concern for individuality is legitimate. There do seem to be strong forces at work in the best and freest of human societies that, when unchecked, stifle the uniqueness of persons, promote conformity, and lead to artistic, intellectual, and social sterility. Thus there are times when rebellion against the prevailing moral views of society is of benefit not only to the individual but to society itself.

St. Francis shocked the moral sensibilities of his time by giving up the wealth and comfort of his upper middle class life to embrace a life of poverty. Many respected people, including his own father, denounced him as shiftless and irresponsible. Yet by persevering in his "madness," he gave the world a luminous example of how to live in imitation of Christ, and changed the whole moral focus of his time. Albert Schweitzer incurred the moral indignation of many by choosing to serve the natives in the African jungle rather than continue exercising his scholarly and artistic gifts. Yet today his life is regarded as a model of service to mankind. Society judged both men crazy. And society was wrong.

Some Feelings Are Wrong

Countless other examples like St. Francis and Schweitzer might be cited to show that the feelings, desires, and preferences of certain men and women are wiser than the prevailing wisdom. Yet we still cannot declare that everyone's feelings, desires, and preferences are unassailable. If they were, then we would have no basis for denouncing tyrants, no rationale for condemning the actions of psychopaths. For not only does every great person and every saint go against society's rules, but so does every mugger, every wife-beater, every child-molester.

Hitler presumably was following his feelings and expressing his deepest desires when he literally exterminated more than six million Jews. Stalin presumably was exercising his preference when he massacred several million peasants. The common spiritual ancestor of both, Genghis Khan, must have achieved emotional satisfaction as he led his hordes across Asia and into Europe, plundering, raping, and devastating. And in our day Charles Manson was following his feelings when he directed his ghoulish followers in their bloodbaths. In each case, these men were merely "doing their thing."

Some time ago, in Nassau County, New York, a homosexual ring of at least 45 members was uncovered. Some members were adults, but many were boys from ages 7 to 17. Most of the boys were fatherless and had been seduced into homosexuality with gifts. If they threatened to report the ring to the authorities, they were threatened with beatings and even death. The adults involved, of course, were not only feeding their desires, but doing so in an enterprising way.[1]

Now, if no individual's view were better than any other's, if everything were a matter of individual preference, then we would have no choice but to *approve* the actions of all these people. And yet no reasonable person would think of approving them. Those actions are intolerable. They are moral atrocities that cry out for condemnation. They are evil. And the feelings, desires, and preferences that spawned them are, therefore, *wrong!*

A Better Guide Needed

When we are thinking clearly and being honest with ourselves, we realize that there is a potential in each of us for noble actions of high purpose and honor; but there is also a potential for great mischief and wickedness. Each of us is capable of a wide range of deeds, some that we would be proud if the whole world knew, and others that, if discovered by a single other person, would cause us shame.

A working woman passing a department store late at night may have a sudden urge to smash the window and steal the mink coat she lusts after. A man may want to seduce his best friend's wife. A student may feel like spreading a lie about his roommate to avenge a real or imagined wrong. A bank employee may have the desire and even a plan to embezzle a million dollars and depart for the South Seas. Each of us, however placid our nature, may on occasion experience an overwhelming urge to punch someone in the nose. Yet each of these actions is at least of questionable rightness, *despite* the feelings and desires of the person.

Similarly, a person walking alone on the shore of a lake may prefer to ignore the call for help that comes from the water. A surgeon relaxing at home may prefer not to answer the call to perform emergency surgery. The father who promised to take his children on a picnic may prefer to play golf with his friends. A lawyer may prefer not to spend the necessary time preparing for the defense of his client. But in such situations the answer, "whatever the person prefers to do is right to do" is hollow. Good sense suggests that the right action may be at odds with the individual's preference.

Since feelings, desires, and preferences can be either beneficial or harmful, noble or ignoble, praiseworthy or damnable, they are obviously not accurate tools for analysis of moral issues or trustworthy guides to action. They themselves need to be evaluated and judged. They need to be measured against some standard that will reveal their quality. To make them the basis of our moral decisions is to ignore those needs and accept them uncritically as the measure of their own worth.

INQUIRIES

1 A little league baseball coach anticipates a poor season because he lacks a competent pitcher. Just before the season begins, a new family moves

into his neighborhood. The coach discovers that one of the boys in the family is an excellent pitcher, but that he is over the age limit for little league participation. Because the family is not known in the area, the coach is sure he can use the boy without being discovered. He wants a winning season very much, for himself and for his team. Is he morally justified in using the boy?

2   Ralph, a college student, borrows his roommate's car to drive to his aunt's funeral. On the way back he falls asleep at the wheel, veers off the road, and rolls down an embankment. Though he emerges unhurt, the car is a total wreck. Since the car is five years old, the roommate has no collision insurance. Ralph is sorry about the accident, but feels no responsibility for paying his roommate what the car was worth. Does he have any moral responsibility to do so?

3   The owner of a roadside restaurant prefers not to serve black customers. He paid for the property, he reasons, and has spent many years developing the business; therefore, he should have the right to decide whom he serves. Is his white-only preference ethically defensible?

4   A small city has a zoning ordinance. The spirit of that ordinance clearly prohibits the operating of a business in areas designated "residential." However, the wording is such that a loophole exists. One man wishes to open a pet shop in the basement of his split-level home. The law is in his favor. Is morality?

5   The executives of three large appliance companies get together to discuss their competitive situation. Among them they account for 91 percent of the U.S. production of their particular products. They decide that by stabilizing their prices, they can benefit their stockholders, invest more money in product research, and thereby deliver a better product to the consumer. They agree to consult one another before setting prices, and to price comparable models at the same price. Is this action ethically acceptable?

6   A man buys a house and later realizes he has paid too much money

for it. In fact, he has been badly cheated. There is a bad leak in the cellar and through one wall, the furnace is not functioning properly, and the well is dry at certain times during the year. The cost of putting these things right will be prohibitive. He wants to "unload" the house as soon as possible, and he prefers to increase his chances of recovering his investment by concealing the truth about the house's condition. Is it right for him to do so?

7 For over half a century a funeral home in Charlotte, North Carolina displayed an embalmed human body in a glass showcase. The body was that of a carnival worker who was killed in a fight in 1911. The man's father, also a carnival worker, paid part of the funeral costs and asked the funeral home director to keep the body until he returned. Nothing more was heard from him. Thus the body, clad only in a loincloth, remained on display for 61 years. Public clamor in 1972 resulted in its removal from public view. The present funeral home director, however (the son of the original director), allegedly felt nothing was wrong in exhibiting the body, which he compared to a mummy in a museum.[2] Is his feeling ethically sound?

6

Is the basis of morality, then, each person's own conscience?

FOLLOWING CONSCIENCE is much more reasonable than following feelings or desires or preferences. For conscience implies some test of behavior more critical than our inclinations.

However, "conscience" is one of those terms we take a little too much for granted. Familiarity breeds, in this case, thoughtlessness. What precisely is conscience? How does it originate? How does it develop? How trustworthy is it as a guide? These pertinent questions are too often overlooked when we speak of conscience.

Conscience is a sense of right and wrong, a sensitivity to moral situations. It is a "still, small voice" that offers us guidance in the choice between alternative actions. Like "mind," it is a faculty or capacity. It has no *physical* reality. It doesn't exist in any place in our bodies. It can't be dissected and examined as our physical organs can. The name we give it and all the references we make to it are therefore metaphorical. We speak *as if* it had a physical existence, as if it "acted" in a material sense.

It is no less real, of course, because we can only speak of it metaphorically. But there are certain limitations in our knowledge of it, certain unavoidable inaccuracies when we speak of it. We can know it only through the thoughts, moods, reactions we experience. When we feel a sense of guilt, we say, "My conscience is bothering me." When we feel blameless in our behavior, we say, "My consience is clear." There is nothing wrong with such expressions—as long as we do not forget that we are speaking metaphorically. By forgetting that, we are likely to ascribe to conscience an infallibility that, as we shall see, it does not have.

The intensity of conscience differs from person to person. Even as small children most of us have perceived, however vaguely, that our playmates and relatives appear to differ widely in this phenomenon we can speak of only obliquely. Preschoolers will often grab toys away from others. And some never show (and if externals are a mirror to internal states of mind, never *feel*) the slightest remorse. Yet others will be so aware of the offensiveness of such behavior that they will immediately be so saddened, so repentant, that their faces will reflect clearly the wretchedness they feel. Hours later they will still be trying to make amends.

The classmates of a grade school stutterer will vary greatly in their attitude toward him. Many will treat him as a nonperson, an object to tease and taunt and mimic. Some will simply know no better, and will be unaware that their actions are wrong. Others will at some moment sense they have caused him pain and will feel ashamed of their behavior.

Such differences in conscience are observable in adults as well. Some people are very sensitive to the effects of their actions, acutely aware when they have done wrong. Others are relatively insensitive, unconscious of their offenses, free from feelings of remorse. They live their lives uninterested in self-examination or self-criticism, seldom even considering whether something *should* be done. Others see right and wrong as applying to only a limited number of matters—sexual behavior, for example, and deportment within the family. The affairs of citizenship and business or professional conduct are, to them, outside the sphere of morality. Still others were at one time morally sensitive, but have succeeded in neutralizing the promptings of conscience with elaborate rationalizations. When Claude's wife expresses disapproval of his cramming the hotel's soap and towels and rugs and bedspreads into his suitcase, he says, "Look, the hotels in this country expect you to take a few souvenirs. They build the cost into their room rates. And if there is a bit more taken than they've allowed for, they write it off on their tax returns."

Finally, there are the extremists: the scrupulous and the lax. Scrupulous people are morally sensitive beyond reasonableness, often to the point of compulsion. They see moral faults where there are none. Every action, however trivial—whether to peel the potatoes or cook them whole, whether to polish the car today or tomorrow—is an excruciating moral dilemma. And their counterparts at the other pole are virtually without conscience, using other people as things, unmindful of their status as persons, pursuing only what satisfies the almighty *me*.

The Sources of Conscience

The kind of conscience we have, the scope of its influence on our behavior, and its intensity, derive from three sources. The first and most obvious is our own conscious moral direction. In this sense, our values are self-determined, freely chosen independently of other influences. It is this sense we are most aware of. When we behave in a certain way, we are usually quite confident that we have a choice, that we are choosing, and that there is no influence operating on our behavior but what we freely *will*. This is much less often the case, however, than most of us are aware. More often, the two other sources influence the development and action of our conscience significantly.

One of these sources is natural endowment. A person's basic temperament and level and kind of intelligence are largely "in the genes." And that temperament and intelligence play a considerable role in the shaping of the total personality. The person with a practical intelligence and the one with a philosophic intelligence will not have the same potential for ethical analysis, nor the same potential for perceptiveness in moral issues. This is not to say that the two kinds of intelligence are mutually exclusive. Some people, happily, have both. There are, after all, philosophers of science and philosophers of technology; and the contributions of mathematicians to modern philosophy have been considerable. Neither is it to say that those with more philosophical potential always use that potential, or that this factor is always so dominant as to make them have more developed consciences. It is to say that the kind of intelligence one has, like the degree of intelligence, opens some doors of potentiality and closes others. Similarly, the basic temperament, largely a matter of one's metabolism, poses certain obstacles and opportunities in the development of conscience.

For example, the vivacious, energetic person, quick of movement and speech, who constantly performs in metabolic overdrive, may tend to be somewhat less disposed to careful analysis of past actions than the slower, more reflective person. The impulsive person, impatient to do and have done, may be virtually incapable of prior reflection. Conscience, in his case, may operate only after the fact. It is not, of course, a matter of one disposition, one metabolic rate being preferable to another. Each presents some fertile areas for the development and use of conscience, and some barren ones.

The other source of conscience is the most neglected. Yet ironically, it is in many ways the most important. It is *conditioning*, the myriad effects of our environment—the people, places, institutions, ideas, and values we are exposed to as we grow and develop. We are conditioned first by our early social and religious training from parents. This influence may be partly conscious and partly unconscious on their part, and indirect as well as direct. It is so pervasive that all our later attitudes—political, economic, sociological, psychological, theological—in some way bear its imprint.

If a child is brought up in an ethnocentric environment—that is, one in which the group (race, nationality, culture, or special value system) believes it is superior to others—research shows he will tend to be less tolerant than other people. More specifically, he will tend to make hard right-wrong, good-bad classifications. If he cannot identify with a group, he must oppose it. In addition, he will tend to need an "out-group," some outsiders whom he can blame for real and imagined wrongs. This in turn makes it difficult or impossible for him to identify with humanity as a whole or to achieve undistorted understanding of others.[1]

In addition, the ethnocentric person shows, even as a child, an inability to deal with complex situations. The result is that the very ways such a person learns to see and think about his daily affairs with people and ideas follow the path of oversimplification. His way of thinking demands simple solutions to problems, even to problems which do not admit of simple solutions.[2]

The influence of such training on conscience is obvious. And though few of us are subjected to a purely ethnocentric environment as children, elements of it are common in most environments in one way or another. And the effects on us, though less dramatic and pronounced, are nevertheless real and a significant shaping force on our conscience.

We are also conditioned by our encounters with brothers, sisters, relatives, friends. We see a brother or sister's observance or disregard of family rules or his habit of lying to parents. An uncle brings a present he has stolen from work. Our playmates cheat in games. More important, we see not only these actions, but the reactions of the people themselves and of others who observe them. We are witness to all the moral contradictions, all the petty hypocrisies of those around us. We act ourselves, now in observance of some parental rule, then against another, and we sense pleasure or pain. We imitate others' strategies for justifying questionable behavior.

Next we are conditioned by our experiences in grade school, by our widening circle of acquaintances, and by our beginning contact with institutional religion. We perceive similarities and differences in the attitudes of our teachers and classmates. We observe their behavior, form impressions, sense (quite subliminally and vaguely, to be sure) the level and development of their consciences. We meet and learn from our priest, minister, or rabbi. And perhaps in all these situations it is not the formal so much as the informal contact, the mere introduction to their personalities, habits, patterns of behavior that affects us in dramatic, though subconscious, ways. Memory clouds, experience remains indelible.

We are then conditioned by our contact with people, places, and ideas, through books, TV, newspapers, and magazines. Day after day, year after year, the contact expands—from the quiz show and soap opera we watch with our mother when we come home from school, to the evening news, to the situation comedy that suggests, on occasion, the response of laughter to situations we were taught to deplore, to the forbidden books and magazines we nervously study in the suspicious quiet of our rooms. Through experiences numerous beyond calculation and varied beyond recall, our views are by turns confused and made clear, our parental teachings challenged and reinforced.

But always we learn. We develop. And our conscience is shaped.

Finally, we are conditioned by the individuals and groups that fill our teenage and young adult years. Our teachers from junior high school through college influence us. So do our associations in boy scouts or girl scouts, little leagues, service clubs, interscholastic sports, cheerleading, twirling, church youth groups. Later we may be conditioned by membership in fraternities or sororities, political and social clubs.

These, then, are the three sources of conscience: our own creative efforts, our genes, our conditioning. The order, of course, is not chronological. However early and forceful our first efforts at shaping our own conscience may be, they are preceded by the shaping force of heredity and by years of conditioning. Whatever is possible in the way of self-direction—and whatever our situation, the potentialities are large—there are limits that have been set by those prior influences. And in the case of conditioning, at least, the influence continues. Today is different from yesterday. Our general routine may be the same, we may operate within the same few miles of space. Yet the specific experiences are constantly changing, and constantly working subtle changes in us. At no point in our lives can we say our conscience is completely under our direction.

Going Beyond Conscience

The idea that the only source of conscience is our self-determined choice of values is an illusion. And any honest effort to enlarge our ethical perspective must begin in the rejection of that illusion. Conscience is important. Indeed, it is the most important single criterion of right and wrong we have as individuals. It is, as the saying goes, the "proximate norm of morality." Yet, alas, it is not completely reliable. It is subject to many influences, most of them subtle, and represents at best an imperfect level of moral awareness.

We must follow our conscience: the only alternative is to violate it, and that would be worse. It would, at the very least, lead us to neurosis. But we cannot *just* follow it. To do that is to remain, in part, prisoners of circumstance.

54

True freedom, true individuality, and real moral growth lie in questioning conscience, evaluating its promptings, purging it of bad influences and error, guiding it with searching ethical inquiry and penetrating ethical judgment.

For our purposes in examining moral issues in this and subsequent chapters, the answer "It's a matter for the individual's conscience to decide" will be inappropriate. Let's consider a few cases to see exactly why. A high school girl hears a rumor that a classmate is a shoplifter. Is she morally justified in repeating the story to her best friend if she makes her promise not to "tell a soul"? A 13-year-old boy walks into his neighborhood grocery store and asks the grocer for a pack of cigarettes "for my mother." The grocer knows the mother doesn't smoke and that the boy is too young to buy cigarattes legally. Should he sell them to him? A weapons manufacturer has an opportunity to make a big and very profitable sale to the ruler of a small foreign country. He knows the ruler is a tyrant who oppresses his people and governs by terror. Is it right for him to sell the weapons? A college girl's friends are all sleeping with their boyfriends and are urging her to "loosen up" and follow their example. (Her boyfriend is not opposed to the idea.) She can't decide, and the more she ponders the matter, the more confused she gets. What should she do?

Whatever we decide is right in these cases, we should go beyond leaving the matter to the individual's conscience. If we say that in the first three cases, we are saying, in effect, "Any action is acceptable." For we can have no way of knowing exactly what those people's consciences will prompt them to do. And if we said it in the case of the college girl, we would be evading the issue; for her dilemma is deciding whether the promptings of her conscience are reasonable.

INQUIRIES

1 For each of the following cases, decide whether the person's conscience was correct. That is, decide whether the action it directed him to take (or silently approved) is ethically justifiable. Explain your reasoning.

(a) Broderick stops at a pay phone to make a call. As he is talking, he absentmindedly fingers the coin return and finds a dime someone has carelessly forgotten. When he is finished talking, he pockets the coin and walks away. Halfway down the block, he feels guilty for taking it. He returns to the booth and deposits it in the coin return.

(b) A doctor is driving down the highway late at night. He sees a car in the opposite lane swerve sharply off the road and plunge down an embankment. No other cars are around. His first impulse as a physician is to stop and assist the victims. However, he remembers that the state has no "good samaritan law" to protect him from a malpractice lawsuit. His conscience tells him he is justified in driving on.

(c) A middle-aged candidate for the local school board is running against a 25-year-old man. He has heard the rumor that his young opponent gives "wild parties." As he proceeds with his campaign, he visits the homes of many voters. He makes it a point to tell everyone what he has heard about his opponent, always adding, "Of course, it's only a rumor that no one has yet proven to be true." He believes sincerely that it would be dishonest of him not to inform them about the rumor, so that they can evaluate it before voting.

(d) A professor in graduate school has several student assistants, talented young men and women pursuing doctorates. He regularly uses their research findings in his own scholarly writing, without crediting them either in the text of his articles and books or in the footnotes. "It's part of their job to do research for me," he reasons; "the money they receive from their fellowships for doing the research is credit enough." His conscience does not trouble him.

(e)   In order to beat out the competition for a summer handyman's job at a nearby estate, Alan agreed to work for a wage somewhat lower than the standard of the area. The owner and his family are at the estate only on weekends and Alan works alone. Though his work-day is fixed—9 to 5, Monday through Friday—he arrives late and leaves early on most days and occasionally takes an afternoon off. He does not feel guilty because his employer is paying him less than others would have worked for.

(f)   An enterprising black real estate broker hires a white man and woman to buy a house in a white neighborhood and then transfer title to him. He then visits the white residents of the neighborhood and explains that he owns one house already and plans to buy others and sell them to black families. He tells each white resident that some other white neighbor has secretly agreed to sell. Everyone becomes frightened that property values will plummet and many are tricked into selling to the broker at much lower prices than their homes are worth. The broker then sells the homes to black families for what they are really worth. Not only does he feel morally blameless, but he regards himself as a hero of sorts, a fighter against discrimination in housing.

(g)   Fred is the oldest of seven children of a widow. He is an honor student in a technical program at a nearby junior college. He pays his way by stealing automobile tires, radios, and stereo tape decks, and selling them. When he first took up this part-time "occupation," he felt a little guilty. But he no longer does, for he decided that no one is really injured: the owners will be somewhat inconvenienced, but not deprived, because their insurance will cover replacement costs.

2   The following people all have clear consciences. Decide whether they are entitled to and explain your decision.

(a)   George believes strongly that drug use and dealing are a personal matter, outside the sphere of morality. He sells marijuana, pills, cocaine, heroin, anything. Whatever there is a market for, he will deal in.

(**b**) Gus specializes in LSD, which he laces liberally with strychnine to increase his profits.

(**c**) Mary Jane sells marijuana.

(**d**) Sam believes strongly that the use of any drug is a crutch and that hard drugs ruin lives. He volunteers to be an undercover agent at his college, without pay.

3 The consciences of the people in the following cases are confused. As a result, the people cannot decide whether the actions they are contemplating are morally right. Decide for them and present the rationale for your position.

(**a**) A married couple discover that their 22-year-old daughter, a college senior, is an active lesbian. They are shocked and dismayed, for they regard this as moral degeneracy. They are thinking of refusing to attend her graduation and refusing to welcome her in their home until she renounces this way of life.

(**b**) A student is taking a composition course in college. Her assignment is to write on the morality of the Vietnam War. Back in her room she moans aloud that she doesn't know where to begin with such a complex and large subject. One of her roommates declares where she stands on the issue. The other challenges her view. In time, several students wander into the room and get involved in the ensuing discussion. One goes out and gets a term paper she did on a similar subject. She reads it aloud, and is interrupted from time to time as someone disputes a statement or expands upon it. After an hour or so, the session breaks up, leaving the girl who didn't know where to begin with a different problem: deciding to what extent, if any, she is justified in using in her paper the facts and opinions she heard from the others.

(c) Harry has been a patrolman in the police department of his small city for a year. He has seen many violations of department policy: squad car teams who regularly pull off on lonely streets and sleep during evening shifts, patrolmen receiving "quiet money" from gamblers and dope pushers, officers conducting sexual commerce with women in the station house while on duty, sergeants and lieutenants spending whole shifts at home and altering duty records to cover their absence. Harry is seriously considering turning these men in, but is confused about where his loyalty should lie.

(d) An airline pilot goes for his regular medical checkup. The doctor discovers that he has developed a heart murmur. The pilot has only a month to go before he is eligible for retirement. The doctor knows this, and wonders whether, under these unusual circumstances, he is justified in withholding the information about the pilot's condition.

If the majority isn't necessarily right, feelings can be capricious, and conscience is imperfect, how can the moral quality of an action be determined?

AT THIS POINT in our search for a basis for evaluating moral issues, we may feel a sense of frustration and even of futility. Particularly if our ethical stance was anchored to one of the standards we have found insufficient, we may feel adrift and insecure. We may even be led to conclude that no basis is available.

But let's reflect on what we've discarded. Are the positions "The majority must be right," "Trust your feelings," and "Follow your conscience" the expressions of individuality? No. They are rather the expressions of a misunderstanding of individuality. They confuse individuality with unwitting, uncritical dependence on others' views, or on our conditioning, which amounts to much the same thing. The conclusions such positions lead us to in moral issues are not judgments; they are easy substitutes for judgment. And though they have value in their place, when taken out of their place, and made to substitute for judgment, they are more than conditioned reflexes, like the droolings of Pavlov's dog.

To develop a sound and meaningful basis for discussing moral issues we must find some definition of right and wrong, moral and immoral, that is acceptable to men and women whose moral perspectives and the ethical systems they lead to differ greatly. In other words, that definition must shun the differences among ethical theories and embrace the similarities. By proceeding from those considerations that are fundamental to all, or least most, ethical systems, we can set aside our normal defensiveness about our own positions, free ourselves from the entanglements of prefabricated interpretations, and elevate our dialogue to a more analytic and objective level.

The Common Concerns

One concern common to all ethical theories (save perhaps the most esoteric) is with the way human relationships affect the quality of moral actions. Every significant human action occurs, directly or indirectly, in a context of relationships with others. And relationships usually imply *obligations*; that is, restrictions on our behavior, demands to do something or avoid doing it. The most obvious kind of obligation is a formal agreement. Whenever a person enters into a contract with someone—for example, to sell something or to perform a service—we consider him ethically (as well as legally) bound to live up to his agreement.

There are other kinds of obligations too. There are obligations of friendship, which demand, for example, the keeping of confidences. There are obligations of citizenship which, in a democracy, demand concern for the conduct of government, and responsible participation in the electoral process. There are business obligations. The employer or supervisor, for example, is morally bound to use fair hiring practices, judge his workers impartially, and pay them a reasonable wage that is consistent with the demands of their position and the quality of their work. The employee, in turn, is morally bound to do his job as efficiently and competently as he is able to. And both have moral obligations to their customers.

In addition, there are professional obligations. The lawyer is obligated to protect the interests of his client, the doctor to promote or restore the health of his patient, the teacher to advance the knowledge and wisdom of his students, the elected official to serve the interests of his constituents.

When we say obligations bind morally, we mean they exist to be honored. To honor them is right; to dishonor them, wrong. (The fact that an obligation may be found to be illegitimate does not refute this idea. An illegitimate obligation is a contradiction in terms: if it is illegitimate, then it is not an obligation.) Even if the action we are required or forbidden to perform is morally insignificant, the obligation has moral force. Thus, if Edna promises not to go to the carnival without notifying Carl in advance, to break the promise is to do wrong. Now surely there is nothing wrong in going to the carnival or in not calling Carl beforehand. It is the *promise* that binds Edna.[1]

A second concern common to virtually all ethical systems is with the way actions serve or violate important *ideals,* such as tolerance, compassion, loyalty, forgiveness, brotherhood, peace, and especially respect for persons, justice, and fairness. Since such ideals are notions of excellence, goals that bring greater harmony in one's self and others, it is understandable that they are a natural part of ethical thinking in every time and place.

Different cultures interpret the same ideal differently, of course. And, as we have seen, the way a culture interprets its ideals and relates one to another will affect its judgment of particular actions. The Eskimo accepts the ideal of respect for the aged, but some of his ways of honoring it—for instance, walling them up in an igloo to die when they are too old to contribute to the community and are a drain on its resources—are somewhat different from ours. And the same ideal of justice that we honor may impel someone in some culture to do something we would never think of doing; for instance, to cut out the tongue of one who has uttered a taboo word. These variations in the ways of viewing and pursuing ideals surely pose exquisite dilemmas for those engaged in cross-cultural studies and those whose occupations involve them directly with other cultures (diplomats, for example, and medical and religious missionaries). But they present less difficulty for us in the examination of our own culture.

A third and certainly most important consideration is with the *consequences* of the action—the effects that flow from it and affect the people involved. We can agree to call "good" those actions which benefit people, and "bad" those which bring them harm. The benefit or harm may be physical or emotional. It may occur immediately or at some later time. It may be consciously intended by the person who performs the act, or completely unintended. And it may be obvious or very subtle and quite contrary to appearances. Because the effects of actions can be complex and difficult to pinpoint, ethical analysis very often requires not an examination of indisputable facts, but speculation about possibilities and probabilities.

How to Proceed

On examining a moral issue, the first step is to identify the important considerations involved: Are there any obligations? What human ideal or ideals does the action relate to? Who are affected by the action? In what ways are they affected? The next step is to decide where the emphasis should lie among the three considerations. Sometimes the issue will be mainly a matter of obligation; at other times the ideal will be most important; at still other times, the consequences. Not infrequently, the force of all three will be very nearly equal.

Let's consider a few moral issues and apply this approach. Agatha, a married woman with three children, is in the habit of seeing her unmarried minister alone rather often. Since the relationship began several years ago in a mutual interest in intellectual and social issues, it has grown and expanded. There has been no overt sexual dimension to the affair; it is strictly platonic. Nevertheless, her daily visits to his home and his frequent visits to hers, sometimes when her husband is at home, but often when he is not, are the subject of community gossip. Is it morally wrong for Agatha to continue the relationship?

There are several obligations involved. As a wife, Agatha has an obligation to her husband (as he does to her) to build and nurture a mutually satisfying physical and emotional relationship. As a mother she has an obligation to provide a home and atmosphere conducive to her children's physical, emotional, moral, and intellectual development. The minister too has at least one obligation—to serve his congregation's religious and spiritual needs.

At least two ideals are involved: marital fidelity, and honesty with self and friends. (We might also note the traditional but now frequently questioned ideal of the minister as a model of scandal-free behavior.) Marital fidelity has, of course, more dimensions than the sexual: a spouse can be faithful in body but not in mind, in attitude, in heart. The ideal of honesty with selves, each other, and others permits no deception about the depth and quality of the relationship.

What about the consequences of continuing the relationship? It is unlikely that Agatha's marriage will be strengthened by it, her relationship with her husband improved. In fact, the reverse effect is a distinct possibility. The effect on the husband is likely to be embarrassment and shame if he is aware of the gossip about his wife. Even if he is unaware of it, the fact of his wife's attentions to the minister and neglect of him will be a source of anxiety and pain to him. And though the children themselves may not be neglected by their mother and may remain ignorant of the precise cause of the tension between their parents, they will surely not be benefited by the existence of that tension.

In this case the three considerations are of nearly equal force. All of them considered, we might well conclude that it is wrong for Agatha to continue the relationship, that despite the satisfaction she and the minister get from it, and despite the fact that it is not tainted by sexual infidelity, it does cause harm. If she still loves her husband, the right action would be to end the relationship with the minister. If she no longer loves him, and sees no hope for rekindling love, it would be to leave him.

Let's turn to a very different situation. Mr. Barker is returning to a town he once lived in and a position he once held. He and his wife visit several real estate brokers there in hopes of finding a house. One broker mentions that Mr. Dumbrowski's house will soon be for sale. "Oh," the man says, "I know Dumbrowski; is he leaving the area?" She explains that he is not, but is moving to a house she showed him, a larger house because his family has outgrown their present home. As they are driving to inspect the Dumbrowski property, the man casually asks the broker which house Dumbrowski is buying. The broker tells him. She innocently adds that he is paying $18,000 for it.

After leaving the broker, Barker goes directly to the owner of the house Dumbrowski is planning to buy, inspects it, is impressed with what he sees, and says to the owner, "Look, I know Dumbrowski has offered you $18,000.

I'll pay $19,000, and what's more, you won't have to pay any broker's commission.'' The owner agrees and Barker buys the house. Was Barker's behavior unethical?

Whether Barker triggered a legal obligation between the broker and the owner of the house is a difficult question. (That question hinges on whether she had mentioned the property to him in her capacity as real estate broker. The fact that she answered, as he asked, casually and as if the property were no longer for sale, clouds the issue of legality.) Did he violate a moral obligation? Clearly, she did not give him the information so that he could use it against her interests. She trusted him and he used the information in a way that injured her financially. The issue comes down to whether we are *obligated* not to act on information someone carelessly gives us. It may be tempting to say yes, but it is not reasonable. Whatever we wish he had done, or conclude he should have done, we cannot make the case on the basis of obligation.

What ideals are involved? The obvious one is fairness. The action most in keeping with this ideal would be for Barker to have refused to take advantage of his knowledge about the house, to have considered it sold to Dumbrowski and not interfere. But at very least, if he felt impelled to outbid Dumbrowski, he could have approached the owner in such a way that the broker's commission would be paid. After all, without her help, however inadvertently it was given, he would not have known about the property.

The effects of Barker's action are plain enough. The broker lost the commission. Dumbrowski and his family lost the house they almost bought. But these effects, though unfortunate, are not *in themselves* sufficiently harmful to make the action wrong. In this situation, then, the three considerations are not equal. What makes Barker's behavior wrong is not any breach of obligation nor the harm of the effects in themselves. It is his failure to honor the ideal of fairness.

Morality Defined

The definition of "right" and "wrong" which we will use in future chapters and inquiries will reflect the three considerations: the *obligations* that derive from the relationships, the *ideals* involved, and the *consequences* of the action in question. Any action that passes scrutiny in these matters we will call "right" or "moral." Any action that is found wanting we will call "wrong" or "immoral."

INQUIRIES

For each of the following cases, determine the obligations, ideals, and consequences and in light of those considerations decide whether the action is right or wrong.

1   A seventh grade teacher divides her class into teams to research some history topics and report to the class. Each team consists of four students. One team of four girls presents a report that is excellent in substance. However, two members of the team behave childishly in making their contributions, so the overall presentation is flawed. The teacher lowers the team's mark a full letter grade. Since the grade recorded for each team member is identical to the team grade, each of the four girls is penalized.

2   A businessman is waiting for an elevator in his office building. A stranger motions him aside and whispers, "Wanna buy a fur coat for your wife? $200. No questions asked. What say?" He opens a large paper bag to reveal the coat. The businessman looks at it, touches it, and realizes that the coat is unquestionably mink and worth at least 10 times what the man is asking for it. He takes out his wallet, hands over the 200 dollars, and takes the bag.

3   A common method for dispatching animals in slaughterhouses is to hit them on the head with a sledgehammer as many times as necessary to drive them into semiconsciousness, then to impale one of their rear legs, hoist them into the air, and slit their throats, leaving them to bleed to death.

4   A woman learns that her son-in-law fathered an illegitimate child several years before he met her daughter. (He and his wife have been happily married for 10 years. They are childless.) She is sure her daughter is not aware of this and has reason to doubt that she would ever find out about it by herself. The woman feels obliged to tell her, however, and does so.

5   The executives of a large company are planning their advertising campaign for the coming year. They would prefer to use a simple and honest approach, but they know that their competitors use devious psychological approaches and even outright lies in their advertising. They fear that if they do not use the same approaches as their competitors, their company's profits will suffer and they may lose their jobs. They decide to play it safe and use those approaches.

6   A boy and girl, both college students, have been living together off campus for three years. They have never considered marrying and it has always been implicit in their relationship that each should be free to leave the other any time he or she wishes. Unexpectedly, she becomes pregnant. Since she is opposed to abortion, she resigns herself to having the child. When she is seven months pregnant, he decides to leave her. One day when she is out shopping for groceries, he gathers his belongings, scribbles a hasty note ("Our thing was real great, but, now, somehow, it's, like, empty.") and leaves.

7   The scene is a large room at a political convention. The members of a state delegation are entering to caucus about an important issue. The meeting is closed to the public and press. However, one enterprising reporter has anticipated the caucus and is carrying forged credentials identifying him as a member of the delegation. Hoping for a news scoop, he flashes his false credentials at the door, moves inside the room, flips on his concealed tape recorder, and mingles with the crowd.

8   A businessman wishes to invest some money in wooded land. He knows that he can sell the trees for lumber, plant more trees, and sell them when they mature. He will be serving the cause of ecology at the same time he makes a modest income. After finding a parcel of land that is appropriate for his purposes, he asks the owner the selling price. The price is so ridiculously low that the man realizes the owner is unaware of the value of the trees as lumber. He ponders whether it is immoral to buy the land at such a price. He decides it is not, and buys it.

9 A young woman has a serious kidney disease. She undergoes expensive care while awaiting the availability of a donor's kidney. One day she receives word that a donor has been found. She looks forward happily to the transplant operation. Then she finds out that the donor is an institutionalized mental defective who is unable to understand the nature of the operation and the remote possible danger to him should his other kidney ever become damaged. The surgeon will be removing the organ without his permission. The young woman accepts the kidney anyway.

10 Knowing that after negotiations with management are completed they will get less than they ask for in wages and fringe benefits, some labor unions begin negotiations by demanding more than is reasonable.

11 Allegedly, the U.S. Army is researching mechanical ways to control human behavior. For example, they are conducting experiments with devices that use "flickering light of varying intensity" to render the brain incapable of controlling the body, and devices that emit audible sound to confuse the mind and cause pain. (An Army spokesman stated that such devices might be useful in controlling crowds.)[2]

12 A newspaper boy begins his job with enthusiasm. His supervisor explains that once or twice a week, advertising inserts will be delivered with the papers and must be placed inside them. The job of inserting is a time-consuming chore, the man explains, and paperboys are easily tempted to discard the inserts. However, he warns, discarding them is grounds for dismissal, because the advertisers pay for them and have a right to expect them to reach the customers. Not only is each newspaper boy expected to handle his own inserts properly, he is also expected to report any other paperboy who does not do so. Two weeks later, the boy notices that all the other delivery boys in his town regularly throw the inserts in a trash barrel. He reports them to his supervisor.

13 Midwestern University is a national football power. The alumni association, which exerts considerable influence on the university's affairs, does not tolerate losing teams nor any faculty member or administrator who stands in the way of victory. This year Professor Woebegone has had the misfortune of having Roger Rapid, star halfback, in his mathematics class. Roger is mathematically illiterate. After spending many extra hours with Roger in hopes of dragging him through the course successfully, Professor Woebegone has been forced to admit failure. On the final exam Roger has scored 27. Judged by the grading scale in the course, his final average is an F. Yet since he is a borderline student in other courses, an F will surely place him on academic probation and he will be ineligible for the last crucial game of the season. Without him the team will surely lose the conference title. Professor Woebegone, who is untenured, may well lose his job. The professor turns in a D+ grade for Roger.

Darling,
The day wouldn't be
important without you —
Love, Bill

8

What do we do in situations where there is more than a single obligation? How can we reconcile conflicting obligations?

IN THE LAST CHAPTER we mentioned a number of obligations, all of them deriving from some formal bond of faith to people or institutions. In addition to such obligations of fidelity, British ethicist W. D. Ross has suggested four other types: obligations of *reparation,* making amends for the wrongs we commit and their effects; obligations of *gratitude,* demonstrating our appreciation for the considerateness of others; obligations of *justice,* giving to others what they deserve; and obligations of *beneficence,* doing good acts for their own sake.[1]

Any one of these obligations may be present by itself in a moral situation. But more often two or more are present; and many times they conflict. In such cases the problem is to choose wisely among them.

The executives of a corporation, for example, must make a difficult decision. Their profit picture has been dismal. If they do not find some way to cut back their expenses, they may be driven into bankruptcy. Since their biggest expense is salaries, it is clear they must make economies there. After analyzing the various operations of the corporation, they determine that they can effect significant economies by curtailing certain services to customers and combining the work of three departments.

This reorganization will make it possible to reduce the work staff by 12 people and result in savings of tens of thousands of dollars. However, each of the people involved has been employed by the company for more than

15 years, and all are between ages 45 and 55. They are too young for retirement and too old to find other positions very easily.

The dilemma the executives face is the conflict between their obligation to old and faithful employees and their obligation to stockholders. Both obligations demand fulfillment. Both obviously cannot be fulfilled. There may be some middle ground possible—some special waiving of the retirement rules that will permit some at least to retire early. But even in cases where the executives have the power to grant such a waiver, it is unlikely that they could do it for all 12 people. Choice is unavoidable. They must give preference to one obligation or the other.

Another very common example of a moral dilemma caused by conflicting obligations is that faced by the person who is asked to give a job reference for a colleague or subordinate whom he believes may not be able to perform the job in question. The chairman of an academic department, for instance, may be called by his counterpart in another school. "I'm calling about an applicant of ours who worked for you until last year," the caller says. "His name is Dr. Elmo Ryan and he's applying for a position in sociology." The chairman winces. He remembers Ryan all too well. For three years the poor man struggled to teach his courses well. The chairman visited his classes and tried to help him improve. Several of his colleagues in the department did likewise. Finally, everyone was driven to the same conclusion that the students who were unfortunate enough to be in his classes had long since reached—he simply was not meant to be a teacher.

Now the chairman must answer a direct question about him to a prospective employer. If he tells him the truth about Ryan—that he is a hard-working, personable, cooperative *incompetent*—Ryan will surely lose the job. He feels a certain obligation to Ryan. And yet he feels obliged to the man on the phone and to all the students Ryan might be assigned to teach. Whatever the chairman decides to do, the decision will not be easy. It will require breaking one obligation.

Does everyone have an obligation to assist in the rehabilitation of former thieves and rapists by giving them a chance to return to society without discrimination? Most of us would agree that there is such an obligation, at least one of beneficence. But if a banker thinks to honor that obligation and hire the reformed thief, he must also consider his obligation to his customers and to the Federal Deposit Insurance Corporation to maintain the security of his bank. And if the owner of a girls' camp wishes to honor that obligation and hire the reformed rapist, he must consider his obligation to insure the safety of his clientele.

Weighing the Obligations

In cases where two or more obligations are in conflict for our attention, the best we can do is to *consider the relative importance of each and give preference to the more important one*. To judge well we need a sense of proportion. That is, we need to perceive what balance among the obligations will serve each one to the extent appropriate, and thereby make the best of a bad situation. Whenever both can be partly served, they should be. Whenever only one can, the more important one should be.

If a person owes two hundred dollars to someone who needs the money, and then, just when he is able to pay, he reads in the paper that contributions are being sought for flood relief in a neighboring state, he may be torn between settling his debt and donating to the needy. Which should he do? A rationale could be developed to support either. But a better case could be made for settling his debt. The obligation of justice in this case would be more important than the obligation of beneficence. (It is not necessarily so in every case where two obligations conflict. If the creditor did not need the money immediately and the act of charity were to a family with no income that neither qualified for public assistance nor was likely to find any other private benefactor, beneficence would be more important.)

A merchandiser for a clothing concern is in his busiest season of the year. Moreover, the demands of his job this year are even greater than usual because two very different and daring fashion trends are competing with a well-entrenched mode. The right judgment on his part in assessing the buying public's taste will make a great deal of money for his company; the wrong judgment could ruin them. Meanwhile his wife, whom he loves, is in a state of depression. She feels she has disappointed her husband by being unable to have children, she suspects him (wrongly) of infidelity, and she is given to periods of depression in which she contemplates suicide. The psychiatrist she has been visiting says she is not dangerously ill, but could easily become so. He advises the husband to take her on a month's vacation.

What should the husband do? He owes his employer his expert judgment during the next month. Yet he owes his wife help and attention. Which obligation is greater? Surely we would have to rule in favor of the wife, both because her health is more important than the company's business interests and because the relationship of husband and wife is more important than the relationship of employee to employer.

To the extent possible he should, of course, try to serve both obligations. He might, in other words, postpone the vacation for a week or ten days and during that period work a sixteen or eighteen hour day. He might even take work with him on the vacation or telephone the office every day to provide whatever guidance he could to his employer. But it would be a graver fault to neglect his wife's needs than to neglect his employer's.

Two Legal Dilemmas

Such choices challenge lawyers and doctors virtually every day. Clarence Darrow, the famous attorney, is said to have won a case by stealing the jury's attention during the prosecutor's summation. He smoked a cigar in which he had placed a wire to prevent the ashes from falling. With each puff the ashes would grow longer . . . and the jury would sit a little farther forward on their chairs. When would those ashes fall? They never did. And however brilliant the prosecutor's closing words were, they were ineffective. The jury was too busy watching that cigar to pay any attention to them.

Darrow's bit of vaudeville represented a choice between his obligation to his client and his obligation to courtroom procedure. Obviously, in his judgment no trick was too cheap to play if it helped his client. Was his action morally blameless? Hardly. It was an open and shut case of wrongdoing, though not a particularly damnable one (and one that we would probably be inclined to approve if our life were in the balance).

A similar case of a lawyer forced to choose between obligations occurred more recently in New York City. Martin Erdmann, a Legal Aid Defender, remarked publicly that judgeships today must either be bought or won through political influence. He was brought before the New York City Bar Association for violating the group's code of ethics. (The Association recommended that no action be taken against him.) Now Erdmann had an obligation to the legal profession to conduct himself responsibly. And he had an obligation to that profession, and to the citizens it represents, to speak out against abuses within the profession. Undoubtedly he judged the latter obligation to be more important.

How do we judge his action? To judge fairly we would have to know more than the details given above or available in the news accounts of his case. If the situation concerning the selection of judges is as he described it, then it makes a mockery of our system of jurisprudence and of the very concept of justice. It cries out for denunciation. And his obligation to speak would indeed take precedence over his obligation to be silent. On the other hand, if the situation is not as he described it, or if he wasn't sure and didn't bother to determine the validity of the description, then the obligation to be silent and not scandalize the courts would take precedence. If he had knowledge of some abuses but did not know how widespread they were, the requirement of proportion would have demanded that he modify his statement to reflect his degree of knowledge rather than speak in general terms and indict, by implication, all judges.

The Alabama Syphilis Case

In the summer of 1972 a shocking disclosure was made about a government-sponsored medical experiment that had gone on, unnoticed, for *forty years*. The experiment concerned the effects of syphilis. The Public Health Service began the experiment in Alabama. Its purpose was to determine the extent of the damage that syphilis will do if left untreated. (Its effects, most of them known or at least surmised at the time the experiment was begun, are blindness; deafness; degeneration of the heart, bones, and central nervous system; insanity; and death.) Six hundred black men were selected for the experiment. They were promised free transportation to the hospital, free medical treatment for diseases other than syphilis, and free burial. Apparently they did not receive clear explanations of the possible harm the disease could cause them, if left untreated.

Of the 600, a third never developed syphilis. Half of those who did received the arsenic-mercury treatment that was standard before the discovery of penicillin. The remaining two hundred got no medication. Even after the discovery of penicillin a decade later and its widespread use as a cure for syphilis, they received no treatment. They remained human guinea pigs.

There were several obligations the researchers should have weighed. First there was their obligation as physicians to care for their patients. Then there was their obligation in justice, of respecting other human beings and treating them in a manner consistent with their humanity. Finally, there was their obligation as researchers to serve mankind by seeking cures for deadly diseases. They seem to have ignored the first two completely. Apparently they thought of the men not as patients, but as the "subjects" of the experiment—as phenomena to be studied, rather than as persons to be cured. And if they recognized the inhumanity of their handling of the two hundred men, they failed to act upon their recognition. (There is a bitter irony in this case. During the very period in which the experiment was conducted, Nazi doctors performed similar barbarities on the inmates of concentration camps. After the war, at the Nuremburg trials the United States and our allies condemned those doctors for "crimes against humanity.")

The shock felt by every sensitive person at this disclosure reveals the importance of choosing well between conflicting moral obligations. For it was not wrong for the doctors in the Atlanta case to honor their obligation as researchers. What was wrong was their ignoring the two other obligations, both of which were more important.

INQUIRIES

Identify the conflicting obligations in each of the following cases and decide whether the action taken is right or wrong. Be sure to consider the requirement of proportion.

1 In studying the subculture of a particular group a sociologist must be accepted by the people and gain their trust. One such researcher is studying the people in an urban slum. He learns through their confidence that certain members of the community are involved in a car-theft ring. He does not report them to the police.

2 A Roman Catholic priest disagrees with his church on the issue of abortion. A parishioner comes to him for guidance. He does not mention the church's official position on the subject, but gives her his own moral judgment.

3 A lower-echelon executive of a large company learns that the company is violating the state anti-pollution law by dumping chemicals into the lake bordering their plant. The state inspectors are being bribed to ignore the violation. The executive takes no action.

4 A professor of psychology wishes to learn the effects of various conditions on students' learning. He significantly varies the heat, lighting, noise, and humidity of his classroom during examinations. He also on occasion purposely garbles half a lecture or repeats a previous day's lecture verbatim without comment.

5 A Senator believes strongly that the country has over-subscribed the defense program to the detriment of social services. Yet he is from a state which receives a large number of defense contracts, and if he introduces legislation to curtail defense spending, he is likely to be defeated in the next election. He decides not to introduce it.

6 Daniel Ellsberg was in possession of the classified Pentagon Papers, secret government documents pertaining to the Vietnam War. He released them to the press, and thus revealed their contents to the American people and to the world.

7 A very competent druggist, well-versed in the latest pharmacological studies, receives a prescription from a physician which he recognizes is for a dangerous, highly addictive, and largely discredited medication. He calls the physician and is told curtly to mind his own business. As the customer waits in the front of the store, he ponders the situation. "Should I refuse to fill it? Should I tell the customer I am certain the doctor has made a mistake? Should I call the medical board and report the incident?" He decides to fill the prescription.

8 Claude, a college freshman, learns that his roommate and friend is pushing hard drugs on campus. Claude is not opposed to drug use. He smokes marijuana himself, though has never used any hard drugs. Neither does he believe that drug pushing is wrong. But he does fear for his own safety, since if his friend is discovered and their room searched, his own marijuana might be found. After removing his marijuana from his room, he slips an anonymous note under the dean's door, informing on his roommate.

9 An Old Testament professor in a Protestant seminary does not accept the school's literal interpretation of the Bible. In his classes he introduces his students to a number of philosophies of interpretation, including liberal ones. Learning of this violation of the school's traditional theological perspective, the faculty deliberates at length. Finally they reach a decision. The professor is to be fired.

10 In the summer of 1972 a theoretical physicist in California, Vincent

LoDato, completed his calculations concerning means of controlling thermo-nuclear fusion. He applied for an $80,000 grant from the Atomic Energy Commission to have his equations computer-examined. After reviewing his calculations, the Commission decided that they involved processes useful in controlled nuclear fusion and related to the making of hydrogen bombs. So they stamped every page of his notebook "secret/classified," forced him to withdraw a scientific report he had submitted to a journal for publication, and ordered him to cease working on the subject in question. In effect, in LoDato's judgment, they are forcing him out of that area of research.[2]

11 A doctor on duty in a hospital emergency room one Halloween night treats a 15-year-old-boy whose eye was injured by an exploding firecracker. He notices the boy is drunk. Because the extent of the injury is not certain, he has the boy admitted to the hospital and notifies his parents. When they arrive, the boy is under sedation, so his drunken condition escapes their detection. Nevertheless, the doctor informs them that he had been drinking.

9

How can we reconcile conflicts between ideals or between an ideal and an obligation?

AS HUMAN BEINGS, we learn to live with the limitations of our existence. There are gaps between what we know and what we wish to know about ourselves and the world around us, between what we are and what we might be. And nowhere is the gap wider than between the demands placed upon us by our ideals and the possibilities for fulfilling them. As we noted previously, ideals are by definition lofty goals that in their fullness always exceed our grasp. To complicate matters further, there are many situations where ideals compete.

A kindergarten boy from a poor family rides the school bus to and from school. On the half-hour ride many of the other children on the bus entertain themselves by teasing him about his plain clothes, his unkempt hair, his worn shoes. Day by day the abuse continues, becoming more and more cruel. An 11-year-old girl, sensitive to the feelings of others, notices the boy suffering in silence, unable to understand why the other students want to make him feel bad. The girl is repulsed by his appearance, and is not at all eager to alienate her friends. Honesty bids her stay out of the affair. But kindness prompts her to sit with him, speak with him, become a "big sister" he can look forward to seeing each day on the bus so that the rejection of the others will not scar him emotionally.

By choosing to honor the ideal of kindness, the girl necessarily violates the ideal of honesty. Does she do right? If we believe kindness to be the higher ideal in this situation, we will agree that she does.

An interesting case of conflicting ideals occurred not long ago in the filming of a documentary account of the life of a young evangelist, Marjoe Gortner. The film shows how Marjoe perfected and used his pentecostal pitch on crowds of believers. He didn't believe he was preaching a "miracle of God." In fact, he didn't even believe in God! The producers intended the film to reveal this and thus to serve the ideal of honest reporting. However, in filming the revival meeting scenes they used real revival meetings set up by Marjoe. Thus the crowds who appear on the screen were exploited, their religious beliefs by implication mocked in the film.[1]

Was the use of real believers in real revival meetings morally justified? To decide, we must consider whether the ideal of honesty in reporting outweighed the ideal of respect for the many sincere believers and tolerance of their beliefs. In other words, we must determine which ideal represented the *greater good* (or the lesser evil).

If there had been no way to create a set and use actors, or perhaps if the point of the film had never been made before, then the ideal of honesty in reporting might have taken precedence. But there was a way, and though it would have been more expensive in time and money, the cost would not seem to have been prohibitive. And the point had been made in books and films. Therefore, the offense to the people and the insult to their beliefs outweighed the authenticity achieved. The producers' decision did not represent the greater good.

The Munich Incident

In the summer of 1972 the world shared the dilemma of the West German police officials when Arab guerrillas held members of the Israeli Olympic team hostage and attempted to leave the country with them. The police were faced with the decision of how best to free the Israelis with a minimum of harm to everyone concerned. The ideal of respect for the rights and safety of the victims clashed with the ideal of reverence for the lives of the guerrillas. If the guerrillas were allowed to leave the country with their hostages, the hostages faced almost certain torture and death. Yet if the police tried to prevent them from leaving, the lives of both would be threatened.

The police tried to minimize the danger by tricking the guerrillas, gaining entry to the buildings they had taken over, and subduing them. But after this and other efforts failed and the guerrillas and their captives were at the airport, the police were left with their final plan—to separate the guerrillas, kill their leader, and either overpower the others or persuade them to surrender. The plan, of course, did not work as intended and the Arabs and Israelis were killed when the helicopter exploded.

Was the plan to murder the leader justified? Had it been the first response, it surely would have been questionable. Human life, even the life of a criminal, is a precious thing and should not be treated lightly. But in this case it was a last resort, put into effect only after other less violent actions had failed. And since it was designed to save lives, it was surely justified. The only alternative to it would have been to stand by while many innocent men were taken to their deaths. Was it, then, a desirable action that decent men could be proud of performing? No. But it was the lesser of two evils.

Ideals Versus Obligations

Frequently, ideals compete not with themselves, but with obligations. Every time a policeman takes a gun from a criminal, he is choosing his obligation to prevent crime over the ideal of respecting private property. Every time a doctor prescribes a placebo for his hypochondriac patient, he is placing his obligation to care for his patient over the ideal of honesty. No reasonable person would think of challenging the choices made in such cases. There are situations, however, in which the promptings of ideal and obligation are more nearly balanced.

The body of a man who died from cancer has just been delivered to the funeral parlor. As the undertaker begins to prepare the body for burial, the telephone rings. The caller is the director of a nearby medical school. It seems that the type of cancer the man had is very rare and the opportunity to study it more closely could provide valuable insights in the fight to cure cancer. The director and his staff, as well as the medical staff of the hospital, suggested that the man will his body to the medical center, but he refused. After his death they pleaded with the man's relatives to permit an autopsy. They refused. The purpose of his call, he explains, is to request that the undertaker cooperate with them and permit the autopsy to be made without the relatives' knowledge.

The undertaker is being asked to set aside his obligation to the relatives to treat the body as they wish and honor the ideal of concern for the suffering of his fellow man. If the autopsy were certain to provide needed insights in the study of cancer, we might conclude that he should agree to the autopsy. But since it offers only a possibility, and since his obligation to the family is not casual, but serious and formal, he should refuse.

Consider still another case. Simon's cousin comes to his house one evening and explains that he is in a desperate situation. He has been in debt to loan sharks for some time, and has been able to postpone the due date several times. Now his time is up. He has received the final warning: pay up tonight or die. He must raise $23,000 in five hours. It is futile even to try to raise the money. He could turn himself in to the police, but that would only be a temporary solution. The moment he was released from their custody, his life would again be in jeopardy. All he can hope for is to hide out for a week or 10 days and then attempt to slip out of the country. He begs Simon to hide him in his home for a while.

Simon weighs the matters. He and his cousin have never been close. He hasn't even seen him in 10 years. But the cousin's life is at stake. Simple charity demands that Simon honor his request. On the other hand, if Simon harbors him in his own home he will surely be endangering his wife and children, whom he has an obligation to protect. The men who will be searching for him are not likely to look kindly on witnesses who can identify them. And they are probably not above harming women and children.

Even though he may be virtually sending his cousin to his death, it would be a greater wrong for Simon to endanger his loved ones. It is not necessary that he be certain they will be harmed. The likelihood that they would be is sufficient for Simon to deny his cousin the act of charity.

In summary, then, in cases in which there is a conflict between ideals or between an ideal and an obligation, we should choose the action which will achieve the greater good. Where the choice of actions is such that no good can be achieved, we should choose the action that will result in the lesser evil.

INQUIRIES

In each of the following cases, identify the ideals, or ideals and obligations, that are in conflict. Examine the action taken or proposed and decide whether it achieves the greater good (or lesser harm).

1 Shortly after the Democratic convention of 1972, it was reported that Senator George McGovern's running mate, Senator Thomas Eagleton, had received electric shock treatment for emotional problems. Senator McGovern decided to seek a new running mate.

2 A policeman is on duty in the station house when he overhears the victim of a robbery describing the robber to the desk sergeant. The policeman realizes that the description fits his older brother perfectly. He pretends not to have heard the discussion.

3 Eight-year-old Tom receives a new and expensive toy from his parents for his birthday. They emphasize that they expect him to take special care of it. While playing with his friends, Tom notices that one boy keeps staring at the new toy. Realizing that the boy is poor and would be thrilled to have such a toy, Tom gives it to him to keep.

4 A young policewoman is assigned to plainclothes duty in a local college. She attends classes, lives in a dormitory, and cultivates friendships with

many students. Through those friendships she identifies the campus drug pushers, "sets them up," and arrests them.

5   A team of doctors has been assigned the difficult duty of deciding which of two patients will receive the next heart transplant when a heart is available. The patients are Anne, 12 years old, the only child of a shoemaker and his wife; and Mark, 48, an executive and the father of four children. They choose Anne.

6   An 18-year-old boy, home from college during the semester break, stumbles on the fact that his father, whom he thought to be a business machines salesman, is actually a gunman for the mob. Moreover, that he recently killed a member of a rival mob faction. The boy considers going to the police and turning his father in, but does not do so.

7   Raoul is a private detective. He specializes in cases in which husbands or wives suspect their mates of infidelity. In the performance of his service, he hides microphones in offices and homes (including bedrooms), breaks into homes and searches for incriminating evidence, and steams open private correspondence.

8   Two weeks ago Arthur was hospitalized for a series of tests. Yesterday the doctor called his wife in and explained that he has a fatal disease and has at most six months to live. The doctor adds that, in his judgment, Arthur would experience great difficulty coping with the truth. Today, sensing that something is troubling his wife, Arthur guesses and probes, "You're hiding something, aren't you, Martha? Is it about my tests? Am I going to die?" She has never lied to him and cannot bring herself to lie now. She tells him the truth.

9   Sheena is thirty-five, married and the mother of six children, the oldest of whom is 12. During the past several years she has become increasingly committed to the cause of Women's Liberation. She has just accepted the vice-presidency of a nationwide feminist organization. The job pays no salary

but covers her travel expenses. She will be away from home an average of three days (and nights) each week.

10 Some time ago a man placed an ad in an underground newspaper seeking a young woman who would be willing to become pregnant for a $10,000 fee plus expenses and other benefits. The replies numbered in the thousands. He then explained to those who were interested that he represented a couple who could not have children. The plan was for the husband to impregnate the volunteer and then, nine months later, the couple would adopt the child. Among the reasons offered by the volunteers were the following: (**a**) a divorced woman wanted the money for a down payment on a house, (**b**) a married woman wanted the money to put her husband through school, (**c**) another married woman wanted to supplement the family income, (**d**) a single medical student wanted to finance the remainder of her education.[2] (Consider each volunteer's situation separately.)

11 A psychiatrist has been treating a young man for several months. From the beginning he observed certain homicidal tendencies. During today's visit, the young man is unusually disturbed. He gestures wildly and shouts that soon everything will be all right: he has found out who his persecutors are and will deal with them. The doctor considers having the young man confined in a mental hospital immediately. But he has reason to believe that confinement may worsen his condition, that this crisis does not represent a deterioration of his condition, but a temporary emotional state which will soon pass. So he does not order confinement.

12 A social caseworker learns that one of his clients is secretly playing in a band two nights a week and earning twenty dollars. Since the man is physically disabled and receiving full welfare benefits for himself and his family, he is required by law to surrender any other income to the welfare department. Thus he is breaking the law by keeping the twenty dollars. The caseworker, knowing that the welfare benefits are based on an unrealistically low cost of living index, does not report the man.

13   A man is elected to the presidency of a small country. Soon after his inauguration, he begins quietly to undermine the other branches of government and to assume more and more power himself. Within a few years his control is absolute. A large army and secret police force assure that his will is obeyed. Taxes rise, private businesses are taken over by the government, the standard of living of the average citizen plummets to a mere subsistence level. Protests are met with imprisonment and, in some cases, execution. A small band of men and women assassinate the tyrant and a half dozen of his henchmen.

14   A high school basketball coach has a rule against smoking. Any team member who is caught violating the rule is supposed to be dropped from the team for the remainder of the season. Several days before the big game of the season, the game that will determine the league championship, the coach catches his star player violating the rule. He decides not to suspend him.

15   On October 13, 1972 a plane crashed high in the Andes mountains, killing almost two-thirds of its 45 passengers and crew, and leaving the others exposed to below-zero temperatures and the threat of starvation. Sixty-nine days passed before they were found. After their rescue it was revealed that they had resorted to eating the flesh of their dead companions as a means of survival.[3]

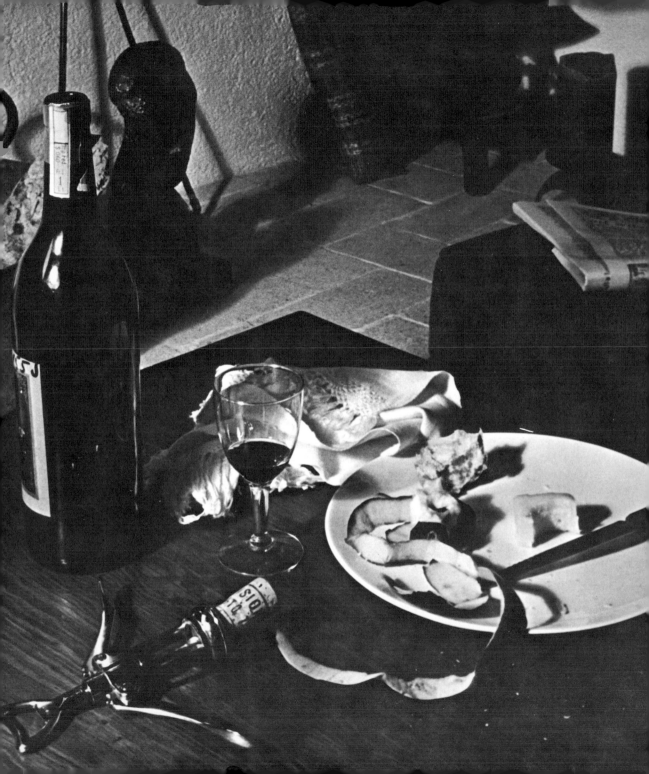

10

How do we deal with cases in which the effects are not neatly separable into good and bad, but are mixed?

ACTIONS IN MORAL SITUATIONS often produce not single effects, but combinations of effects—some good, some harmful. The first step in dealing with such actions is to identify the various effects. More than a cursory examination is needed. If the judgment is to be informed, *all* the effects must be noted: the direct effects on all the people touched by the action; the indirect effects on others; the effects on the person performing the action. The emotional effects must be considered as well as the physical, and the delayed as well as the immediate.

In an earlier inquiry we considered the situation of Fred, the son of the widow with seven children, who pays his way to college by stealing and selling automobile tires, radios, and stereo tape decks. He decided that his behavior is justified because it helps him without hurting others: the owners are a bit inconvenienced, he reasoned, but the insurance companies replace the stolen property.

Fred's examination of the effects of his action was shallow. He recognized only one dimension of one effect. There are other dimensions of that effect, and other effects, to consider. There is the effect on the insurance companies and their stockholders—making them pay for the stolen items. There is the effect on all the people who take out insurance policies with that company—making them pay higher premiums. There is the effect on every citizen's attitudes—contributing to fear and anger and suspicion. Not least there are the effects on Fred himself—reinforcing the habit of solving problems the easy way, blurring his sense of right and wrong, stilling his conscience with excuses and rationalizations.

One of the earliest cases we noted was the poignant case of the young girl who was raised by foster parents from infancy and then, at age nine, returned by court order to the former drug addicts who had neglected her. The effects that must be considered in this situation include those on the real parents, the foster parents, and the girl herself. The effects on the real parents, of course, are beneficial. They gain a purpose for living and for remaining off drugs. They can overcome the terrible sense of loss and of failure that must have plagued them since their child was taken from them. Unfortunately, the foster parents experience almost the opposite effect: a feeling of helplessness, a profound sense of loss, and perhaps a bitterness about the seeming unfairness of the court decision.

The obvious effect on the little girl is sadness and confusion at being separated from the only real parents she has ever known, and at being given, like some inanimate object, to two strangers. But there is also a deeper, delayed effect. Such an experience is sure to leave an emotional scar on her. Will she be made bitter and cynical about human relationships? Will she be driven inward, avoiding the sharing of love and affection with others because of the subconscious fear that they too may be taken from her? Will she be filled with resentment toward her real parents and turn against them and all they try to do for her?

Each of these possibilities is very real. And though there is always the chance that none of them may happen, and instead her suffering may enrich her life and her trauma lead her to become deeply sensitive to the sufferings of others, such a happy ending seems rather unlikely. The effect of lasting emotional damage is more probable. And this most significant effect is the best measure of the morality of the court action.

A careful analysis of effects will thus cover the subtle ones as well as the more obvious. For example, many of those who argue against the brutality of slaughterhouse methods—the pounding of helpless animals into semiconsciousness, the brutal slashing of throats and draining of life—rest their case not on any premise that animals deserve human consideration, but on the idea that *we* are dehumanized by condoning such brutality, that every time we close our eyes to such methods, we quietly assent to the same seed of violence that takes other, more abhorrent forms. Whether such an argument is correct or not is not the issue here. The point is that such an effect is conceivable and it is not to be found on the surface of the issue. It can only be grasped by more painstaking consideration. And many of the moral issues that confront us have similar subtleties to be recognized and dealt with.

When Harm Is Unavoidable

There are situations in which a beneficial effect and a harmful effect are inseparably joined; that is, situations in which either choice will produce an undesired effect as well as a desired one. A congressman, for example, may be encouraged by a big business lobbyist to vote for a bill that is against the interests of his constituents. The lobbyist implies that if the congressman supports the bill, big business will support his campaign for reelection. The congressman knows that he faces a tough campaign against an unprincipled opponent. Without the support or at least the neutrality of big business, he has virtually no chance of reelection.

The harmful effect is unavoidable in this situation. If he votes for the bill, the effect will be harmful to his constituents. But if he votes against it, the effect will be the loss of office to someone who will not serve the interests of those constituents. Would the congressman act unethically by supporting the bill? No. For there is no preferable action open to him. He would not be choosing the harmful effect. He would be merely tolerating it to achieve the good effect.

This idea may seem radical. Actually it is a rather conservative ethical approach. It has, for example, traditionally been applied by Roman Catholic ethicists in cases of fallopian pregnancy. In such abnormal pregnancies, the fetus fails to move down the fallopian tube and lodge in the uterus. Instead it lodges in the fallopian tube itself. If it cannot be dislodged and made to continue on its course to the uterus, it will develop in the tube and cause the woman to hemorrhage and die. Despite the well-known Catholic opposition to induced abortion, in such cases Catholic ethicists approve surgical removal of the nonviable fetus. They reason that the harmful effect of destroying the fetus is inseparable from the good effect of preserving the mother's life.

The Greater Good

In situations involving mixed effects, as in situations involving conflicting ideals, the morally preferable action is the one which will *produce the greater good or the lesser harm.* In the early 1960s a white writer, John Howard Griffin, took a chemical to darken his skin and traveled about the southern U.S. posing as a black man in order to determine what it was like to be black in America. His masquerade resulted in very helpful insights (published in *Black Like Me)* that advanced the cause of civil rights by promoting public awareness of the prevailing racial double standard. Of course, while the study was being conducted, Griffin deceived hundreds, perhaps thousands, of people. The reason the masquerade was ethically acceptable was that the harm it produced was slight in comparison to the good.

Another interesting, if somewhat unusual, example of a "greater good" decision occurred during World War II. In the North African theater of operations many hospitalized soldiers awaited the arrival of the first large shipment of the new wonder drug, penicillin. When it arrived, high military medical officials had to decide which of two groups of patients to use it on, those with infected battle wounds or those with sulfa-resistant gonorrhea. Those with gonorrhea got it. The decision may at first seem absurdly wrong. But consider the reasoning that led to it. Large numbers of gonorrhea victims were crowding hospitals and posing the threat of infection to others. Within a week these men could be returned to the battle lines where, because there was a shortage of manpower and because victory was not yet assured, they were badly needed.[1]

The dilemma facing the medical officials in that case was certainly unfortunate. And the choice they made unquestionably caused harm. But it was undoubtedly the right choice in that situation because the alternative choice would have caused more harm. Giving the penicillin to the V.D. victims served the greater good.

The question of the greater good arises, of course, not only in such peculiar cases as that of Griffin's masquerade and the penicillin dilemma, but in many everyday situations.

After a young college instructor submits his final grades, he receives a stereo album from two of his freshman students with whom he has become quite friendly outside of class. The note accompanying the gift explains that it is a token of their gratitude for presenting such an interesting and meaningful course. Should he keep the gift? It would seem harmless to do so since they obviously offered it in good faith and not as a bribe for better marks. Giving it back or otherwise disposing of it might offend them and injure his friendship with them. Yet accepting it will mix and confuse his two separate roles as teacher and as friend. As teacher, he *owed* them as interesting and mean-ingful a course as he could present. He was paid to present it. If they were to take another course from him, their misunderstanding of his dual role could strain their relationship with him and cause mutual embarrassment. And what of the effect on other students? If they learn that he accepted a gift for doing his job, however small a gift and however innocent the circum-stances, they might lose respect for him. If that happened, his effectiveness as a teacher would be diminished.

The greater good requires that the instructor not accept the album. For-tunately, in this case there is a way of handling the situation so as to minimize the risk of hurting his friends' feelings. After enjoying the album for a few days, he can donate it to the college library or student union, and explain to his friends that though he appreciated the gift, he wanted to avoid setting a precedent that others might misunderstand.

A Caution

As difficult as it is to deal with the observable good and evil effects of already-completed actions, it is even more difficult to consider the effects of contemplated actions or hypothetical actions. Therefore, whenever we deal with the latter kinds of actions it is well to keep the following caution in mind:

However clear and logical our determination of effects may be, it is a prediction of future events, and not a certainty. The particular set of responses that occurs, and the changes in the thoughts, attitudes, and behavior of everyone affected by the action, are intricate and sometimes, in some ways, unpredictable. Thus we are dealing with probabilities at best. For this reason, we must be thorough in accounting for all possible effects and willing to modify our earlier judgments as actual effects become available for our examination.

INQUIRIES

In each of the following cases, identify the various effects of the action taken and decide whether the action represented the greater good.

1   A college instructor is pursuing his doctorate in night school. To gain extra time for his own studies, he gives his students the same lectures, the same assignments, the same examinations year after year, without the slightest effort to improve them.

2   A physician on the staff of an urban medical center is approached by a lawyer from a remote part of the state and asked to testify on behalf of his client, a rural doctor charged with criminal negligence in the care of a patient. The lawyer admits that his client is guilty of the charge. He goes on to explain that, though the doctor is old and not well versed in the latest medical knowledge, he is nevertheless competent; and the negligence he is charged with resulted from the strain of being the only doctor in a large mountain area with a number of tiny towns and a population totalling two thousand people. The lawyer pleads with the medical center physician to testify that the negligent act was proper treatment. The physician does so.

3   John and Martha, both married and the parents of several children, are having an adulterous affair. One night when they are meeting secretly, they witness a murder. They agree they cannot report it without exposing their affair. The next day the body is found and within a week a suspect is apprehended and charged with first degree murder. When John and Martha see his picture in the newspaper, they realize that he is not the murderer. They meet again, discuss their dilemma, and decide that despite the new, dreadful development, they will not step forward as witnesses.

4   For the first time in his twenty years as a high school football coach, Barney Bloom is looking forward with confidence to a winning season. His running back, Phil Blaster, is an athletic phenomenon. He has speed, power, cunning. Then, with practice scheduled to begin in three days, Bloom's bubble bursts. In examining Phil, the team doctor has detected a serious knee condition. His report, backed by a specialist who has studied the x-rays, is that there will be great risk in Phil's playing this season. If the knee sustains a hard jolt from the right angle, Phil may never be able to play football again. Both doctors advise Phil to undergo surgery at once, but they leave the decision to him and his parents. Coach Bloom, determined to have Phil in his lineup, attempts to persuade Phil to wait until the football season is over to have the operation.

5   An English teacher in a two-year technical college has several students in his composition course whose ignorance of the English language has proved invincible. He has given them extra work and extra counseling from the first week of the semester. And they have been diligent in their efforts to improve. Though they are in a construction technology program and will undoubtedly be employed in jobs which require little writing skill, the composition course is required for graduation. In the instructor's judgment, they would not be able to pass the course legitimately if they took it three times. So he raises their F grades to D's.

6   Regina is chairman of her city's United Fund campaign. In her annual meeting with her staff of canvassers, she gives this advice: "Hit the business places first. And don't approach anyone who is walking in a hall by himself or working in a closed office. Look for two or more people standing together or working side by side. Try to make them compete with each other in giving. Capitalize on their desire to show off and outdo the next guy."

7   A senator has a bill before the Senate that promises to correct tax inequities that affect thousands of workers. However, the bill is being held up in committee. The committee chairman is responsible. The senator, however, has learned of a secret scandal in the chairman's personal life. He visits the chairman and tells him that unless the bill is released from committee, he will divulge the scandal to the press.

8   By day Sylvester is a high-ranking executive in a leading lingerie company. By night he is a modern Robin Hood. He scales walls and creeps over rooftops to enter the homes of the wealthy and steal cash and valuables. Everything he takes he gives to the poor.

9   In the inquiries on conscience, we considered the case of a middle-aged candidate for the local school board, who was running against a twenty-five year old man. He had heard the rumor that his young opponent gave "wild parties." As he proceeded with his campaign, he visited the homes of many voters. He made it a point to tell everyone what he had heard about his opponent, always adding, "Of course, it's only a rumor that no one has yet proven to be true." Re-examine this case, focusing on the effects of his action.

10   In the inquiries on feelings, desires, and preferences, we considered the case of the Little League baseball coach who discovered a new boy in the neighborhood who was an excellent pitcher, though he was over the age limit for Little League participation. Because the family was not known in the area, the coach was sure he could use the boy without being discovered and insure a winning season for his team. Re-examine this case, focusing on the effects of the action he planned.

11   Todd and Edna have been married for three years. They have had serious personal problems: Edna is a heavy drinker, and Todd cannot keep a job; also, they have bickered and fought constantly since their marriage. Deciding that the way to overcome their problems is to have a child, they stop practicing birth control, and Edna becomes pregnant.

11

How do we determine whether a person is responsible for his immoral actions? Are there degrees of responsibility?

IN CHAPTER 1 WE NOTED that the ethicist, unlike the law enforcer, is not required to answer the question of a person's guilt or innocence in every moral issue he deals with. There are no courts of ethics; hence, there is no formal judgment of persons. Nevertheless, as we also noted, the ethicist is interested in the question of responsibility for actions. And his insights provide guidance even for jurists.

Moral situations, as we have seen, involve choice. Obviously, when a person knows the quality of the action and makes his choice free from any compulsion,[1] he is morally responsible for the action. These favorable circumstances, however, are not always present. And when they are not, the person is not morally responsible. Moral *guilt* can exist only where there is prior knowledge of the wrongness of the action.

The young child who sees one person stab another on television and then, in imitation, picks up a kitchen knife and stabs his sister, and the severely retarded teenager who, while shopping with his mother, steals an expensive watch, are not morally responsible at all. They lack both an understanding of the nature of their behavior and the mental development to make an informed choice.

Neither can we assign blame to the prisoner of war who is tortured into revealing military secrets he swore to keep. Nor to a witness to a crime who does not step forward because the criminal has threatened to harm his wife and children if he does. In both these cases, the men are acting under duress, compelled to behave as they do by forces outside themselves. In other words, they have little or no freedom of choice.

The psychopath's freedom is also restricted, though by forces within rather than outside himself. Accordingly, some of history's most infamous characters may not have been entirely responsible for their actions. Gilles de Rais, for example, the fifteenth-century marshal of France and patron of the arts who ritually murdered as many as two hundred kidnapped children, may have been acting compulsively. And even Adolf Hitler, the man whose record of evil staggers the imagination—nearly ten *million* human beings wantonly exterminated and the entire world plunged into strife and suffering and destruction—may have been to a great extent morally blameless. For the evidence suggests he was emotionally disturbed. (The question of the moral responsibility of those who followed Hitler, or those who supported his gaining and retaining of power, is of course quite another matter.)

The above cases, naturally, are not typical. They involve a complete or near-complete lack of responsibility. In most moral situations the person acting has some knowledge of the quality of the act and at least some freedom of choice. The decision as to moral responsibility in such cases depends on the *degree* of that understanding and the *degree* of freedom of choice.

Consider this case. A neurotically insecure woman constantly seeks reassurance that she is attractive and desirable. As a result, she is very vulnerable to selfish, insensitive men. When, as happens frequently, a man uses her for his sexual pleasure and then casts her aside, the rejection makes her all the more insecure, all the more anxious to prove her attractiveness, and all the more vulnerable to other men. Two of the men who have used her in this manner are a bartender at one of her haunts and her psychiatrist. The bartender didn't understand her problem. He saw her merely as a pretty and available woman. So he fed her a few drinks and a few smiling lies, enjoyed himself, and assumed that she did likewise.

The psychiatrist, on the other hand, knew her condition very well. He also knew exactly what harm such experiences had on her emotionally. And yet, like the bartender, he calculated and carried out his sexual conquest.

Assuming that neither man acted compulsively, which was more blameworthy? The psychiatrist. Even though he used the woman no differently from the bartender, he understood the effects of his action more fully. He knew the harm he was causing.

The same kind of distinctions can be made with freedom of choice. On the same day in the same area of the same war, three soldiers may perform an identical act, each of them killing an unarmed, unthreatening civilian. And yet differing circumstances may absolve one, partly absolve the other, and damn the third. The first, for example, may have been ordered directly by an officer to shoot the civilian or be shot himself; the second may have received the order indirectly and, not being observed, have had a reasonable chance to disobey without threat to his own life; the third may have killed for pleasure. Our assignment of moral responsibility would be in proportion to the degree of freedom of each man's choice.

Heroism Not Required

In considering the question of moral blame, we should keep in mind that we can be good men and women without being heroes. It is desirable, naturally, to aim for the highest and noblest actions. But there is no moral requirement to do so. The only requirement implied in the concept of morality is to do good and avoid doing evil.

A case in point occurred during World War II. Soon after the Nazis occupied Austria, they drafted Austrian men into their armed services. One citizen they called was Franz Jägerstatter, a simple, uneducated man in his mid-thirties with a wife and young children. Because he believed that Hitler's cause "offended God," he was convinced that it would be morally wrong for him to serve it. So he refused to be drafted. As a result, he was imprisoned. For months his friends, his parish priest, and even his bishop urged him to think of his family and reconsider his decision. They explained that in such a situation, he was being forced to serve and not doing so voluntarily, so he would not be guilty of any wrongdoing. Despite their pleading, Jägerstatter remained steadfast in his conviction. Finally, he was executed.

Did he do wrong? Of course not. His loyalty to his convictions was admirable. He was a hero. But his friends' advice was not wrong either. They and the many who yielded to the Nazi pressure and answered the draft call were weaker than Jägerstatter. They lacked his courage. Yet they were not blameworthy because they did not choose freely.

Conscience also complicates the determination of guilt and innocence slightly. A person, we observed earlier, must follow his conscience and therefore cannot be condemned for doing what it bids him. And yet conscience is an imperfect guide, capable of directing one to wrong as well as right behavior. It would appear, then, that it is not fair to blame a person for doing any wrong act that his conscience supports. Most ethicists would accept this conclusion, provided two conditions were met: (a) the person did not neglect the job of developing his conscience in a responsible way; (b) he did nothing to desensitize his conscience.

In considering the question of a person's moral responsibility, we should keep one fact in mind. *The moral guilt or innocence of the individual has no bearing on the moral quality of the act.* However insane and therefore innocent the tyrants of the world may be, their actions remain barbaric.

INQUIRIES

1 For a group of people to stand by without intervening as a man beats a woman into unconsciousness and then kicks her brutally would surely be immoral. But the moral responsibility of the crowd would depend on a number of considerations. Determine the degree of the crowd's responsibility in each of the following variations.

(a) The crowd is composed of very old men and women. The assailant is young, strong, and armed with an iron pipe.

(b) The crowd is composed of young women, aged twenty to thirty. The assailant is unarmed.

(c) The crowd is a group of construction workers. The man is spindly, middle-aged, and unarmed.

2 A college basketball team is heavily favored to win the forthcoming end-of-season tournament. Then the star player signs a professional contract and is no longer eligible to play with his team. Was his signing unethical? If so, what circumstances would lessen his responsibility?

3 The evidence that smoking is harmful to one's health continues to grow. Now smoking is not only linked to lung cancer, emphysema, and certain heart and artery conditions, but to cancer of the bladder and of the pancreas. With this fact in mind, decide whether each of the following people commits any moral wrong, and if so, identify the circumstances in which he would be morally responsible.

(a) The heavy cigarette smoker

(b) The smoker who encourages a nonsmoker to start smoking

(c) The farmer who grows tobacco

(d) The cigarette distributor

(e) The advertising man who creates ads to entice people into buying cigarettes

(f) The well-known personality who lends his name to cigarette advertising

4 Is heroin-pushing a moral offense? If so, is the moral responsibility

of the heroin-using pusher any different from that of the nonusing pusher?

5 Louise is an investigator for the Internal Revenue Service. Her job consists of closely examining the tax returns of individuals selected at random by a computer. When she finds significant errors in the returns, she assigns penalities. Because the majority of the cases she handles involve middle-income families and because it is her strong conviction that the tax law discriminates against such people she has begun to feel guilty for doing her job. Nevertheless she refuses to quit. Is she doing wrong? If so, what is the degree of her moral responsibility?

6 A high school girl accuses a boy in her class of putting his hand up her dress. The boy is reported to the principal. The principal questions the boy and the girl. He must make his decision on these facts: there were no witnesses, the boy denies having touched the girl, the girl has made similar unsupported charges about other boys in the past. The principal is reasonably sure the boy is innocent. Nevertheless he suspends him from school. Clearly, the principal has acted dishonestly. Speculate on the circumstances that might have been present to diminish his moral responsibility for his action.

Are there any more solid rules of behavior than the ones we've considered, any unchanging truths to guide us?

Generalizations are necessary in ethics. They permit us to get beyond mere feelings, desires, and preferences. They provide a guide to conscience and a standard for moral judgments. Yet a narrow focus on ethical generalizing can close our minds to the complexity of issues.

Whenever we begin an analysis of a particular situation by asserting an unqualified general rule, such as "It is always wrong to take what does not belong to us," we have judged the situation even before we have begun to examine it. For the statement means that every case of such taking is wrong, *including the one we are considering*. And the very act of making the statement saps our curiosity about the issue, just as knowing the answer to a math problem takes away our concern for the calculations that lead to it, or as being told the outcome of a suspense story takes away our interest in finishing it.

Why ponder a problem for which we already have the answer? We may, of course, proceed to consider and judge the facts of the case at hand. But that activity becomes little more than an exercise of form. Like the juror who makes up his mind that the defendant is guilty the moment he sees him, we may appear to be weighing the evidence, and may even believe we are. Yet, in fact, we will already have made up our minds.

But don't such generalizations apply in most cases? Certainly. And that is just the problem. The generalization about the wrongness of taking what doesn't belong to us would cover numerous situations from bank robbery to embezzlement to stealing hubcaps, and even to pocketing the extra change the supermarket cashier gave us by mistake. But it doesn't cover the exceptions, such as finding some change in a public telephone booth, or taking in a stray dog and (after advertising in the local paper and not finding the owner) keeping it. And in judging any particular case we must be concerned with precisely that: whether there is anything about the case that makes it the exception to the rule.

It is tempting to protest that there must be some generalization that applies in all cases. "Do unto others as you would have them do unto you," comes to mind. What, after all, is more basic to morality than this Golden Rule found in virtually all advanced moral systems? And yet, as Paul A. Freund has pointed out, even this rule has its exception: for a masochist's application of it would prompt him to torture others.[1]

Similarly, unqualified endorsement of the idea of personal freedom can blind us to situations where two or more freedoms conflict. Stirred by such a conviction and hearing that a teacher was fired because of his homosexuality, we might rage against the decision. "Injustice," we'd cry. "The man's inalienable rights have been violated." Yet that would not be the most sensible response. It would be far wiser to inquire into the circumstances of the case. If he was fired from a college position merely because he was living in homosexual liaison with another man, then the decision would surely be unjust. But if he was fired from a high school position because he was propagandizing for homosexuality in the classroom, then his release would not necessarily be unjust. And if he was fired from a grade school position for enticing his own students, no reasonable person could quarrel with the decision.

The Willowbrook Incident

An interesting illustration of the danger of relying on sweeping ethical generalizations and the importance of inquiring into the circumstances of the case occurred some years ago. In Willowbrook State Hospital, an institution for the retarded, medical doctors intentionally infected entering children with infectious hepatitis virus. At first consideration, such behavior seems outrageous. It calls to mind the barbarisms of Nazi concentration camps. In fact, not a few critics regarded the action as precisely such a moral atrocity.

The details of the situation, however, undermine that hasty judgment. It was known that a mild form of hepatitis was rife in the institution. Historical data showed that most of the newly admitted children would be infected by natural means. By deliberately infecting newly admitted patients, the doctors could assure them a milder case of the disease, and they could be given special housing and care while ill. Moreover, the plan had been reviewed and approved by several agencies and parental consent was obtained before a child was infected.[2]

The tendency to respond to issues with unqualified generalizations, though natural enough, should not be indulged. The people we are writing for or speaking with deserve better from us. And every important ethical issue demands our careful attention not only to its similarity to other issues, but also to its dissimilarity, to its uniqueness. To give less, to merely mouth an overall, ready-made response is not to use moral rules, but to be used by them; not to be guided by our experience, but to be controlled by it. It takes wisdom to know when the case at hand fits the rule and when it is the exception to it. Such wisdom does not come easily. And if we substitute generalization for analysis, it does not come at all.

Helpful Generalization

There is, however, a kind of generalization that is helpful, that assists us in avoiding both uncritical acceptance of any answer, on the one hand, and over-positiveness in answering, on the other. That kind of generalization does not say to us "Here is the answer: look no further." It does not substitute for analysis and judgment. Rather, it opens avenues of inquiry and stimulates our thinking. Though it may suggest answers to issues, it never imposes them on us in particular cases.

In the preceding chapters we have been developing four such generalizations, four moral principles, though we have not yet given them that name. Here they are, in summary, together with the qualifications we added to them:

1 Obligations should be followed. When two or more obligations are in conflict, we should choose the more important one.

2 Ideals should be served. When they conflict among themselves or with obligations, we should choose the action which does the greater good.

3 Harmful actions should be avoided and beneficial ones achieved. However, harm may be tolerated if it is unavoidable; that is, if it is inseparable from good. Where the effects are mixed, we should choose the action that achieves the greater good or the lesser harm.

4 The person and his action are separate. Our judgments of them should also be separate.

To these principles we must add one other. Nowhere have we considered it in itself. Nevertheless it has been implied in all our discussions. It underlay the treatment of obligations, it was referred to under ideals, and it was suggested in the treatment of effects of actions. It is the principle of *respect for human beings*. This principle places three requirements on us. In the words of Errol E. Harris, they are:

> First, that each and every person should be regarded as worthy of sympathetic consideration, and should be so treated; Secondly, that no person should be regarded by another as a mere possession; or used as a mere instrument, or treated as a mere obstacle, to another's satisfaction; and Thirdly, that persons are not and ought never to be treated in any undertaking as mere expendables.[3]

There are other principles that are useful. And there is a wealth of literature offering interpretation, commentary, and debate of ethical matters. These principles, however, are the basic ones. They provide a sound foundation for all ethical inquiry. Whoever masters them is guaranteed a deeper understanding of the moral issues of our time and a meaningful contribution to the growing discussion of them.

INQUIRIES

1   A Christian missionary is sent to preach the Gospel to a newly discovered tribe. After arriving in their primitive jungle settlement and establishing a friendly relationship with them, he learns that they encourage extramarital promiscuity. He believes that this is morally wrong. He therefore explains to them that such promiscuity is immoral, an offense against God. Is his action ethical?

2   The same Christian missionary next learns that once each year, as an inducement to the god of the hunt to smile upon their efforts, they cut off someone's right hand. (Whose right hand is determined quite democratically, by lottery.) The missionary is appalled by this custom and explains to the tribe that it is based on pure superstition. Is the missionary's action justifiable?

3   The missionary now makes an even more startling discovery. Since they believe women are inferior to men and a tribe with a large number of women is an outrage to the god of good sense, they strictly control the female population. Whenever the number of girl babies exceeds the percentage approved by the wise men of the tribe, they permit no more girl babies born that year to live. More specifically, they take newborn babies out into the wilderness to die. The missionary tries to persuade them that such behavior is wrong. Is this action justifiable? Does your answer to this question agree with your answers to the first two questions? If not, explain why.

4   Arthur's daughter, age twenty, is a junior in college. She decides to live off campus with a male classmate. Arthur disapproves of this arrangement and tells her bluntly, "Stop shacking up or I stop supporting you." Is Arthur's position morally justified?

5 Jake runs a delicatessen in a high-crime section of a large city. After being robbed at gunpoint eight times in the past two years, Jake obtained a pistol permit and bought a pistol. Yesterday a man entered the store brandishing a knife and demanded all the money in the cash register. Jake moved to the cash register as if planning to open it. Then he quickly grabbed the gun hanging under it and, without warning, shot the man six times in the chest. Did he do wrong? Why or why not?

6 Elvira is very much in love with her fiance Ethelred. Though they have been engaged for over a year (and sexually intimate for almost as long), Ethelred balks at setting a date for the marriage. Elvira is convinced that his obstacle is not disaffection, but fear; and that once he can be moved to action, he will be relieved and happy. She therefore feigns pregnancy and plans to feign a miscarriage after they are married. Comment on the morality of her action.

7 A businessman realizes that with the local college enrollment burgeoning, an investment in a trailer court will be profitable. It happens, too, that a perfect site is available. The one complication is that the owner of the land, who lives across the highway, would not sell it if he knew it would be put to such use. The businessman therefore pays a young married couple to buy it for him. They approach the owner, explain that they want the land to build a home on, and even show him fake building plans. Then, after he sells it to them, they turn it over to the businessman. Comment on the morality of this action.

8 Residents of a poor neighborhood are plagued with a drug problem. Five pushers operate openly on their streets and brazenly try to entice their children to take "free samples." A committee of residents has approached the police and begged them to arrest the pushers, but they have done nothing. There is reason to believe some of the police are sharing in the proceeds of the drug trade. The residents decide that their only hope for a safe and decent neighborhood for their children is to take the law into their own hands. Accordingly, one calm summer night they unceremoniously execute the five pushers. Is their behavior morally justified?

9 Hospital workers in a large urban area feel that they are not being paid enough and that their fringe benefits are substandard. They decide to strike. Taking advantage of the special need for their services during holiday periods, they plan the strike to take place ten days before a major holiday weekend. This timing, they expect, will pressure hospital management to meet their demands. Discuss the morality of this strike.

10 Many countries employ secret agents, spies whose duty it is to learn the military or diplomatic secrets of other countries. Is it ethically permissible to work as a secret agent? Is it permissible to be a double agent (that is, an agent who works for both sides while pretending to work only for each)?

11 There are over four hundred pet cemeteries in the United States. People spend from $30 to several hundred dollars—in rare cases, thousands of dollars—to lay their "cats, dogs, parakeets and canaries, rabbits, goldfish and guinea pigs" to rest.[4] Discuss the morality of this practice.

12 Answer each of the following questions in light of the five principles presented in the chapter. Make your responses as detailed as necessary to deal with the various circumstances that could be present and the complexities involved.

(a) Does a man who goes berserk and kills a stranger have any moral responsibility to the man's family? When he recovers from his mental condition is he obligated to them in any special way?

(b) Is it ever morally right for a U.S. citizen to travel to a country with whom we are at war and to tape record criticisms of our government to be broadcast over the enemy radio network to U.S. toops?

(c) Is it morally permissible to drive after having one drink? Two? Three? After how many drinks would it be wrong to drive?

(d) Is it ethical for a person to smoke?

(e) Is it ethical for a person to take habit-forming drugs?

(f) Is it wrong to use a substance (for example, marijuana) for which the evidence is not yet conclusive and which might be harmful?

(g) Does a rich person have, by virtue of his wealth, any special ethical obligation?

(h) Does a genius have, by virtue of his intellectual gifts, any special ethical obligation?

(i) Is drag racing on the highway ethical?

(j) Is it morally right to put old people in institutions when their children have room for them in their homes?

(k) Is it permissible to kill animals of an endangered species?

(l) Is divorce ethical? Is remarriage after divorce?

Contemporary

Ethical

Controversies

BECAUSE THE MORAL ISSUES that follow in this section are among the most controversial and complex of our day, and therefore likely to trigger strong emotional responses, before turning to them it is well to pause and reflect on the implications of the first twelve chapters, and on the lessons that were undoubtedly underlined in your class discussions of the end-of-chapter inquiries. The following ideas summarize the more important of those implications and lessons.

1 *It is important to recognize our predispositions and not allow them to close our minds.* A controversial issue is by definition one in which there are sharp differences of viewpoint. Most controversial issues we are more or less familiar with, at least in outline. We have heard arguments for one side or both sides and, depending on our habits of mind, some will attract and others repel us. It would be unrealistic to expect ourselves to empty our minds and hearts of our prior experiences and observations. But we can examine our minds, recognize the way they have been conditioned to react to the issue in question, and consciously strive to make room for new and different thoughts—at least long enough to appraise their worth fairly.

This does not mean that we should abandon those convictions grounded in experience and careful reflection. It means only that we should distingush between such convictions and casual opinions. That is not always easy to do. For many times the latter will have equal or even greater force in our thoughts. It is an unusual person who has not on occasion found himself taking a firm and unyielding position on a matter he is quite ignorant about. It also means that we can allow our convictions to be tested against new considerations. If they are worthy, they will withstand the test; if they are not, we profit from finding them out.

If all ethical discussion amounts to is a firing of a barrage of our assertions, followed by ducking and reloading as the other person returns fire, then it is of little value. It leads not to understanding, wisdom, and mutual growth, but rather to misunderstanding, tension, and hostility. If debating an issue means no more than unleashing our reflex responses, then it is pointless. It is a foolish person who says, in effect, "What's the issue? OK, then, here's the answer, so don't waste time disputing it." He is "playing God," pretending omniscience.

2 *Forming ethical judgments carefully is half the task; the other half is testing and refining them.* The problem in any analytic task is to stretch our perspective, to make the effort to transcend our limitations. Every technique we can employ to achieve this deepens our perceptions and improves the quality of our judgments. Therefore, avoiding casual generalizations and resisting the temptation to wallow in our predispositions will certainly help us get beyond the superficial. But often more is needed. And more can be done.

After we have worked out what we believe is a sound answer, we can appraise its quality by asking the hard questions: Have I really considered both sides of the issue? Have I been deceived by appearances? Have I oversimplified any part of the issue? Sometimes it is helpful to imagine someone who disagrees with our view challenging it: What points in our view are most vulnerable to criticism? What questions would he ask? What assertions would he make to counter ours?

If we can bring ourselves to answer such questions honestly and completely, and undertake the revision our answers suggest is desirable, we can improve our analyses, sometimes dramatically.

3 *To be an effective writer or conversationalist on ethical issues, we must have a sense of proportion.* A sense of proportion is an awareness of what is relevant to an issue and what is not, what is more and what is less important. There is seldom enough time or space at our disposal to probe adequately every aspect of an issue. For this reason, we must be selective in our analysis, focusing on this detail rather than that one, devoting more attention to one consideration than to another. We show a sense of proportion by assigning more space or time to major concerns, less to minor ones, and omitting trivial matters altogether, no matter how interesting they may be in themselves.

By observing these ideas in dealing with the issues that follow, you will insure more penetrating analyses, more effective delivery of your thoughts to your audience, and more satisfaction to yourself.

Education

1   In education, as in business, mistakes are sometimes made in promoting a person. For example, a respected high school teacher with twenty years of service may be made principal of his school. After serving for a year in this new capacity, the man may have demonstrated clearly that he is incompetent in administrative affairs. But by that time his former teaching position will have been filled. Consider the various ethical considerations involved both in retaining him and firing him, and decide what course of action and what conditions would be the most ethical solution for the school board.

2   Once in a while a case of a teacher who has taught for years with forged credentials comes to light. Once his deception is found out, of course, he is dismissed and may even be prosecuted. But consider the moral dilemma that must exist for the principal when he first learns of the lie. Suppose, for example, the principal learns that instead of having the master's degree the records indicate, the teacher dropped out of college after one year as an undergraduate. And suppose that the teacher is by every measure one of the very best in the school. Should the principal expose the teacher or allow the deception to continue? Would your judgment change if the teacher were not outstanding but merely average?

3 In every academic subject there are areas of controversy, questions which different schools of thought answer differently. For example, in psychology there are Freudian, Jungian, and Adlerian perspectives; in literature there are several approaches to interpretation (such as the esthetic and the psychological). Is it ethically acceptable for an instructor to teach only the school of thought he personally accepts? Would your answer be different in the case of an introductory course than in the case of an advanced course?

4 In determining students' final grades, some college instructors use as one factor their personal, subjective judgment of students' effort and contribution to class discussion. The factor may vary in its weighting from 10 to 20 percent or even higher. Is this practice ethical? Under what conditions, if any?

5 More than a few college professors today believe that the very idea of a grading system is punitive and archaic. Some of them, however, are in the minority at their institutions and are therefore required to submit grades in their courses. One way to do so and still serve their consciences is to give everyone an A, regardless of the quality or quantity of the work he submits. Discuss the morality of this practice.

6 In most colleges the chairman of an academic department is responsible to the academic dean. If the dean should, for example, criticize his department for submitting so many low grades in a particular semester and demand that the department review its grading policy so that it can begin assigning "more reasonable" grades, the chairman would have to decide how to deal with the matter. Each of the following is a possible approach. Evaluate the ethical character of each:

(a) He can call in each faculty member and review his grading policy with him, attempting to determine whether the policy is too stringent.

(b) He can issue a memorandum to the department members explaining the dean's concern and desire that the department grades improve the next semester.

(c) He can issue a demand that each department member's grades conform in the future to the normal distribution curve.

7 Few colleges today are without their experimental courses or curriculums. In their most sophisticated form such courses or curriculums are run side by side with traditional ones so that their effectiveness can be compared. At the outset of such experiments, of course, it is impossible to be certain that the experiment will be even minimally effective. Are such experiments ethically permissible? If so, under what conditions?

8 A teacher is usually assigned to teach courses with specific content. He is expected to select or create lessons that will impart the knowledge and develop the skills that are associated with that content. To do other than that—for example, to teach economics instead of literature in a literature course —would clearly be to break his moral obligation to the students who enrolled for the advertised course. Yet in subtler cases the answer is not so clear. Would it violate that obligation if a chemistry professor presented a filmstrip on chemical weapons as part of an anti-war lecture? Would it violate it if a math instructor spent one class period talking about the importance of population control? Why or why not?

9 Term paper ghostwriting is surely not a new idea. But doing it on the scale of big business, with advertisements in college newspapers, branch offices, and a stable of writers, is. It is possible today to buy a term paper on virtually any subject, complete with footnotes and bibliography. Some companies even offer tailor-made papers. Is such a business ethical?

10 Some time ago a young man filed a one million dollar lawsuit against the high school that graduated him, charging them with legal responsibility for his inability to read and write adequately.[1] It would seem unlikely that the

courts will find the school legally responsible for his ignorance. But is it possible they are morally responsible? Under what conditions might they be?

11   Compulsory education, the required attendance of young people between certain ages (for example, between five and sixteen in many states), has become a tradition in the United States. The idea that requiring young people to attend school is an infringement of their right as citizens, a kind of slavery, is unthinkable to many Americans. Yet there are men and women, some of them respected educators, who are openly expressing that idea. They argue that the child himself, or at least his parents in his behalf, should decide whether he will attend school and, assuming they decide in the affirmative, where, what, and for how long he will study. Consider the ethical side of the question. Are compulsory education laws morally wrong?

12   The age difference between teachers and students is sometimes relatively slight. A first year high school teacher could be 21 and a high school senior seventeen. A college instructor could be 25 and a college senior 22. Would it be in any way unethical for such teachers to date their students? Would it be different if the students were not in their classes?

13   Tenure is the permanent right to a position or an office. In teaching, tenure has traditionally been reserved for those who have proven themselves competent in the classroom. Once it is awarded, usually after a provisional term of from two to five or six years, the teacher may not be fired except for gross negligence of duty or some moral offense. The proponents of tenure have maintained that it frees the teacher from fears of petty pressures inside or outside the school and enables him to function at his creative best. But lately there seem to be a growing number of opponents of tenure. These people contend that it tempts even the best teachers to relax professionally and stifles creativity. What are the ethical considerations that any full discussion of tenure should address, and why are those considerations important?

14   As teachers' unions and professional associations grow in membership, teachers are becoming somewhat more militant and vocal in their demands for salary increases and improved benefits. This process makes the job of the administrator a very delicate one. Understandably, when faced with the annual decision of how to distribute salary increases, many administrators elect wherever possible to divide the money among all teachers rather than single out the most deserving ones. (Having everyone a little happy is less troublesome than having a few thrilled and many angry and questioning.) Which action is the more justifiable ethically? Be sure to consider all aspects, including the effects of each action upon the quality of education.

15 Most teachers' retirement programs calculate the individual's pension based on the average salary earned during his highest earning years. Realizing this, some college presidents routinely promote every faculty member the year before his retirement (whether he meets the established requirements for the rank or not). Thus, the faculty member can get a slightly higher pension. Is this practice of routine promotion ethical?

16 Faced with estimates that by 1980 there will be twice as many trained teachers as there are teaching jobs, many college departments of education are considering curtailing their enrollments. Some critics have opposed such curtailment, arguing that it deprives students of their right to choose their careers. Would such curtailment be morally permissible? Would your judgment be the same for a public college as for a private?

17 Is it ethical for a student not to work to his capacity? Is it ethical for him to study so diligently that he strains the limits of his physical and emotional endurance? Discuss the various degrees of underwork and overwork that occur among college students and decide in what circumstances each becomes a moral issue.

18 The practice of cheating in homework and examinations is probably as old as education itself. And few would deny that it is an unethical practice in most cases. But what of the dilemma of students who do not cheat in their work but know other students who do? Discuss the moral considerations they should make in deciding whether to inform the teacher. And decide when they should, and when they should not, do so.

Media

and the Arts

1   There have been reports that the staff of a popular TV show about the investigative work of a government agency are required to submit all scripts to the agency's director for his prior approval. Any scripts that show his agents making a mistake or using questionable tactics in conducting an investigation are allegedly rejected. If these charges are true, is the agency's action ethical? Is the TV staff ethically justified in cooperating?

2   At various times one or more of the major networks has reportedly outlawed certain subjects and treatments: for example, stories about venereal disease, the portrayal of unmarried couples living together or blacks and whites mingling socially, objective examination of the Vietnam War and the civil rights issue, sympathetic treatment of homosexuals, draft evaders, and militants. Discuss the morality of such censorship.

3   The sponsors of TV shows also can exert influence over the subjects and treatments presented. In some cases they may demand veto power over

scripts, reasoning that since they are paying for the show and their product will be identified with it favorably or unfavorably, they should have the final say about its content. Is it morally right for them to demand this veto power?

4 It is common knowledge that most TV commercials have very little appeal to the mind. They aim for the emotions, and use our hopes and desires and needs to condition us to buy the products they advertise. Do the writers of TV commercials commit any moral offense by these appeals and devices? Do the sponsors by endorsing them? Do the networks by permitting them to be aired?

5 Even a casual viewing of cartoon shows and other children's TV presentations reveals that the numerous and maddeningly frequent commercials used are designed to stimulate the child's normal desire for possessions. Dolls and adventure kits and games are presented in a way that says, tantalizingly, "Look how much fun you'd have, how happy you'd be, if only you owned this." Discuss the morality of such commercials.

6 For a number of years it has been widely recognized that TV has the potential to be the greatest educational device in history. (Not just what is presently considered educational TV, but commercial TV as well.) Does the TV industry have any moral obligation to realize that potential? If so, explain the source of that obligation and the kinds of changes in present programming that would be necessary to realize it.

7 TV news reporting calls for careful editing. Thousands of feet of film must be trimmed to fit a tight time schedule. Events that could not be fully covered in hours must be presented in minutes. Without intending to do so, the men who prepare news broadcasts can distort the news and misinform the viewing public. Do TV networks have any special ethical obligation to insure that such distortion does not occur? If you believe they do, explain why and what kinds of regulations and safeguards would fulfill the obligation.

8 In many newspapers, the letters to the editor column is given more than token space and it becomes a lively forum for a public discussion of timely issues. The number and relative quality of letters published for or against an issue, and even their arrangement on the page, can subtly influence public opinion. Does this power-to-influence carry with it any ethical responsibility? If so, what is it and how can it best be met?

9 Newspapers derive part of their income from taking advertisements for, among other things, movies. Occasionally a paper will set up standards that must be met by movie ads; for example, the stipulation that the ad contain no prurient appeal. Is it ethical for newspapers to exercise such censorship? If you believe it is, do you think that newspapers that do not censor their ads are behaving unethically?

10 In the past couple of presidential campaigns, a number of magazines engaged well-known writers (for example, Norman Mailer, Germaine Greer, and Kurt Vonnegut) to cover and report on the political conventions. Choosing such writers instead of trained political analysts surely adds glamour to the reporting and undoubtedly improves the magazines' circulation. From the financial standpoint, it is an acceptable choice. Is it from the moral standpoint?

11 Newspaper columnists very often are given information which amounts to news scoops. They may be given a copy of a letter or memorandum that incriminates a government official or a political aspirant. The dilemma they must face is to decide whether to publish it quickly so that the public can be informed or to delay publication until the information is verified. Do they have any ethical obligation? If so, how can it be satisfied?

12 Magazine editors are faced regularly with the difficult job of appraising manuscripts submitted by writers. Often they must consider factors other than the quality of the writing. For example, a well-known writer and a relative unknown may submit articles about the same general topic. If the better-known writer's piece is chosen because it is superior, there is no moral issue. Yet sometimes it is chosen even though it is inferior. Under what conditions, if any, would such selection be ethically justifiable?

13 Film studios often buy the movie rights to successful novels. In the process of producing the film, they may make significant changes in plot, characters, and setting. In fact, sometimes the finished film bears little resemblance to the novel. Under what circumstances, if any, is it morally wrong for film makers to alter a novel?

14 It is a psychological truism that everything we say and do, every experience we have, helps to shape us favorably or unfavorably. Children in their formative years are especially vulnerable. Yet certain films, because of their story line, require child actors to portray mentally disturbed, criminal, and even savage characters. Is the use of children in such roles ethically acceptable? If you believe it is sometimes, be sure to specify the conditions that differentiate those situations from unacceptable ones.

15 Is it ethical for an actor or actress to accept a role in a film or TV show, the theme of which he or she finds morally objectionable?

16 Much has been written about the constitutional right of anyone who considers himself an artist to market books or films whose appeal is largely prurient. Are there any situations in which the creation and distribution of such material is ethically wrong? Explain.

17 Most colleges today employ media specialists, men and women who prepare audio-visual aids for teachers. Sometimes these people are given assignments that conflict with their principles. For example, they may be directed to produce for a psychology instructor slides and transparencies that mock their religious beliefs. Is it morally acceptable for them to accept such assignments?

Sex

1   In our culture, fornication (sexual intercourse between unmarried men and women) has traditionally been viewed as immoral. The reasons that have supported this judgment have ranged from religious prohibitions to practical considerations, such as the dangers of pregnancy and of venereal disease. The liberalization of religious views, the improvement of birth control techniques, and the development of antibiotics have resulted in a softening of the traditional judgment. The question of the rightness or wrongness of fornication is seldom hotly debated anymore. Yet it remains a debatable issue. Evaluate the morality of fornication in each of the following situations. If the existence of any special conditions in any of the situations would materially change your judgment, specify those conditions and explain how they would change your judgment:

   (a)   Between two 13-year-olds

   (b)   Between two 17-year-olds

   (c)   Between a 25-year-old man and a 21-year-old woman

   (d)   Between a 25-year-old man and a 13-year-old girl

   (e)   Between a 25-year-old woman and a 13-year-old boy

2   Consider this special, though perhaps not altogether uncommon, case of fornication. A 28-year-old man is engaged. About a month before the wedding he meets an old sweetheart with whom he had been intimate. They have dinner together for old time's sake and recall their relationship. By the end of the evening memory has rekindled passion. They spend the next three days and nights together. Is their fornication ethically justifiable?

3   Some degree of sexual experimentation appears to be a normal part of growing up in our culture. Many teenage boys and girls will indulge in necking and petting (and even intercourse) with partners toward whom they feel only a slight and passing affection. Some, in fact, will on occasion do so with partners they have no feeling for. The sexual activity in such cases is performed not to express love, but to gain experience or to satisy a biological urge. Is there anything morally questionable about this practice?

4   Every campus seems to have at least one nymphomaniac, a girl who has an uncontrollable desire for sexual intercourse and is willing to accommodate a number of men in succession. Whether she is smuggled into the fraternity house window late at night or escorted boldly through the front door of the dormitory, a line of men is usually waiting to greet her. Is it ethically acceptable for them to have intercourse with her? Explain.

5   Sexual promiscuity is frequent indulgence in intercourse with a variety of partners, indiscriminately selected. Is promiscuity immoral? Explain.

6   An unusual case occurred in England some time ago in which a man and his wife were arrested for having sexual intercourse in their yard. Because only a row of flowers separates their yard from their neighbors' and the neighbors' children observed them, the couple was charged with crimes—he with indecent exposure and she with aiding and abetting him. He was found guilty, but she was acquitted after promising not to use the yard for sexual activity again.[1] Was what they did immoral?

7 Like fornication, adultery (sexual intercourse between a man and a woman, one of whom is married) has traditionally been considered immoral. Evaluate the morality of adultery in each of the following cases. If your answer depends on certain conditions, state those conditions.

(a) A married woman whose husband was left impotent after an automobile accident has intercourse two or three times a month with a bachelor who works in her office.

(b) A man is married to a woman whom he loves but who doesn't meet his sexual needs. Since his job takes him out of town two or three times a month, he uses those occasions to find a woman to supplement his sexual activity.

(c) A soldier is fighting overseas for a year. During that time both he and his wife, without telling each other, engage in sexual relations with others.

(d) A "liberated" couple joins a mate-swapping club. They attend club parties together, engage in sexual activities with others, then go home together.

(e) A married man enjoys a good sexual relationship with his wife but has affairs without her knowledge just to add variety and a sense of adventure to his life.

8 Is it ethically justifiable for a married person to decide to become celibate (for, let us say, religious reasons) without consulting his or her spouse? Is it justifiable to do so if he or she consults the spouse and the spouse refuses to consent?

9 Drs. William Masters and Virginia Johnson are well known for their research into human sexuality. The method of treatment which they have found effective in treating couples with sexual problems is a two-week vacation "course." The couple checks into a hotel near the clinic and receives instruction in the therapy technique, which consists of proceeding very slowly from just gently embracing each other during the first few days to intercourse later. Though the explanations are provided in the clinic, all physical contact between the couple is reserved for their hotel room. The therapists do not observe the couple.[2] Are these clinics ethically acceptable?

10 The Masters and Johnson clinics have a number of imitators. One of these is a nude encounter group where men and women with sexual problems meet and learn to perform sexually by experimenting with each other.[3] Is this group ethically acceptable?

11 A number of other sex clinics operate more along the lines of Masters and Johnson, but differ in one respect: they use surrogate partners for single patients. That is, if a single man or woman enrolls in the program for treatment, they provide him or her with a sexually skilled partner. (Masters and Johnson used surrogates in their original clinic, but ceased to do so when their use became controversial.) These partners are paid for their services by the clinic.[4] Is the use of surrogate partners ethically acceptable?

12 The United States plans to send a manned expedition to Mars in 1985. The mission will require two spaceships, each carrying a crew of six. It will take a total of 590 days from blastoff to return. One of the many problems that is as yet unresolved is what to do about the crew's sex drives. NASA psychologists are convinced that homosexual activity will be inevitable unless women crew members are included. (Because of the training and technical competencies required of crew members, it is unlikely that the astronauts' wives would qualify).[5] Would it be morally justifiable to include qualified women to solve the sex drive dilemma?

13 The problem of crew members' sex drives is also a factor in two-month nuclear submarine cruises. It is solved in that case by providing pornography.[6] Is that solution morally acceptable?

14 Legend has it that prostitution is the "world's oldest profession." Some societies have approved it, others have tolerated it, many have tried to eliminate it. Is prostitution immoral in all cases?

15 Our society has traditionally regarded homosexual behavior as a moral abomination. Is it? In answering, comment not only on situations involving consenting adults, but on those involving a consenting adult and a consenting minor. If your answer differs from your answer on the fornication question, explain why.

16 What are the ethical considerations that arise in cases where people undergo sex-changing operations? Are there any situations in which it would not be ethically justifiable to have such an operation?

Government

1   Political campaigns frequently raise the dilemma of to what extent a person is justified in tolerating evil to achieve a good end. A senatorial candidate, for example, may find his staff attacking his opponent with slogans and emotional appeals unrelated to any campaign issue. Is there anything morally offensive in his allowing such methods to continue? If so, are there any special circumstances in which their use would be justified?

2   In order to gain information to help in the election campaign, members of a political party may infiltrate the opposing party. Pretending acceptance of the opposing party's philosophy and the desire to serve, they may attend the convention and try to get as close as possible to the decision-makers, in person or with electronic devices, so that they can inform their own party leaders. Comment on the morality of this practice.

3   The ancient military saying "To the victor belong the spoils" is traditionally applied in politics. A large number of government jobs—at the local and state as at the national level—are appointive. And every time one party is voted out and another voted in, the old appointees step aside and new ones are named, usually from among the ranks of the hardworking party faithful. Examine this practice in light of the principles we have been using.

4 Modern political campaigns are expensive. The cost during a major election year can run into the millions of dollars. The one and five and ten dollar contributions of working people help defray this expense but it is the large contributions of $25,000 and over that pay the big bills. (During a presidential year there are over a hundred such contributors, a few of them giving more than a quarter of a million dollars apiece.) It is understandable that a politician who has been the recipient of a large campaign contribution will be grateful to the donor. It is even understandable that if the donor asked for a favor—say, for the red tape to be cut in the handling of a business license application—the politician would be inclined to intervene on his behalf. Would it be ethical for him to do so? If you believe that a limited amount of "special treatment" would be justifiable, explain where you would draw the line.

5 Some states have rules for all executive and legislative employees whereby they are forbidden to have an interest in business activity which could conflict with their public service, to personally hold any investment in an enterprise about which they might be making decisions as government officials, and to communicate to others any confidential information which would help them gain a business or professional advantage. Are such rules ethically sound? Show how the principles we have been using support or challenge them.

6 Elected officials are sometimes offered special considerations. They may, for instance, be given preferential treatment in obtaining travel accommodations and reductions in fare. When they take a vacation, the hotels and restaurants they visit may discount their bills. Is it morally wrong for them to accept such considerations? Why or why not?

7 Lobbying is a political institution almost as old as government itself. It is the advocacy of a particular interest group's viewpoint, usually by a paid employee. Such an employee, a lobbyist, is registered with the government. His job is to keep the interests of his employers in the attention of the lawmakers, informing them of which bills have the support of his people and which do not, encouraging them to write special legislation, and even suggesting the specific details such legislation might include. Is it ethical to allow lobbying to take place? In what ways and to what extent is it ethically acceptable for legislators to be influenced by lobbyists?

8 Do rich nations have any obligation to help poor nations? If so, in what way and to what extent?

9 Whether or not they have an obligation to help poor nations, rich nations often do help. But sometimes they attach conditions to their aid; that is, they demand the privilege of influencing the poor nation's government or they expect support for their international policies of trade. Is it ethical for rich nations to attach such conditions to their aid?

10 Pollution is threatening our natural resources. Every responsible person wants to protect our planet for the future. Yet the problem is that there are some irresponsible people who care only for the profit or pleasure of the moment. Does the government have any moral obligation to eliminate pollution? If so, identify some ways in which it might fulfill that obligation. (Be sure not to gloss over any moral dilemmas that those ways would cause.)

11 Most countries that have tried to deal with the problem of overpopulation have found that one of the most difficult tasks is to educate the poor to use the techniques according to directions (for example, to take birth control pills each day rather than skip several days). Some of these countries have found it much simpler and more effective to run campaigns urging men and women to submit to sterilization operations. At least one country gave away free transistor radios to anyone who was sterilized. Are such campaigns ethical? Is it morally right for governments to become involved in population control at all?

12 According to the Anti-Slavery Society for the Protection of Human

Rights, "slavery, serfdom, debt bondage, the sale of children, and servile forms of marriage" exist in at least 38 countries in Asia, Africa, and Latin America.[1] Presumably the United States enjoys diplomatic relations and trade with some of these countries. Does the United States have any moral obligation to do something about these practices? If so, what?

13 The ideological differences that have existed among the major world powers for the past several decades have made spying among countries almost inevitable. Though the extent to which the United States practices it is understandably not easily ascertainable, it seems certain that the Central Intelligence Agency is involved in such work in numerous countries around the world. In what circumstances, if any, and to what extent is their spying morally permissible?

14 In their efforts to maintain national security, the Federal Bureau of Investigation has used informants, men and women who make accusations against others or provide the information which supports such accusations. In some cases, informants step forward to assist the FBI in advance and are directed what to learn and how they might go about learning it. In these latter cases, the question often arises, "How far is it ethically permissible for an investigative agency to go in contributing to illegal activities in order to gain evidence to prosecute lawbreakers?" For example, would it be permissible for them to provide (through the informant) the guns, explosives, and vehicles needed to commit the crime? Would it be right for them to permit or encourage the informant to provoke the criminals to commit a more serious crime than they had intended?

15 In 1972 the tomb of an ancient Chinese noblewoman was discovered near the city of Changsha. The remarkable condition of the body, the clothes, and the ornaments of the tomb recalled the greatness of the dynasty to which she belonged, the Han Dynasty that ruled from about 200 B.C. to A.D. 200. Under these rulers, within a single generation wars among numerous territories were quelled; all of what is now China was united under one economic system, one political philosophy, one legal system; roads were built and agricultural reforms introduced. As a result of these stabilizing social changes, the arts and crafts flourished as never before. Yet all these reforms were not introduced democratically; they were forced on the people, often tyrannically. Dissent was not tolerated.[2] Did the positive consequences that resulted justify the methods used to achieve them? Would today's tyranny be morally acceptable if there were a guarantee that it would achieve good?

Business

1   Sometimes a new invention will be viewed as a threat by an industry. For example, if an efficient steam engine were developed for automobiles, the oil industry could anticipate a ruinous decline in gasoline sales. In such cases the industry might be tempted to buy all rights to the invention in order to prevent it from being marketed. Would such a purchase be moral in any circumstances? Explain.

2   In business ventures, timing can often make the difference between success and failure. Occasionally, timing can pose a dilemma for executives. For example, the officers of a company may be formally obligated to consult their stockholders on certain types of policy decisions. Yet situations may arise in which there is no time to consult them. In such situations there is a good chance for the company to profit, but also some risk of loss. Under what conditions, if any, would it be proper for the executives to act without consulting?

3   Drug manufacturers are required to conduct tests on new drugs for a full year to be sure that there are no dangerous side-effects. One relatively small company has had a promising new antibiotic in testing for eight months. There have been no indications of any harmful effects. Now the company learns that a large competitor is about to market a similar drug. They conclude that with a four-month advantage, the competitor will control the market. The small company will be driven out of business. They decide to change the dates on their research and add four months of fake test results so that the antibiotic may be marketed immediately. Discuss the morality of this decision.

4 Barbiturate and amphetamine addiction continues to give cause for national concern. Each year hundreds of thousands of pills manage to slip into the black market and are sold illegally, often to young people. Some observers, including the head of a congressional crime committee that spent two years probing the problem of illegal drug trafficking,[1] believe that the drug manufacturers cannot be blamed if their products are put to illegitimate use. Do drug manufacturers have any moral responsibility to insure that their products are not put to such use?

5 It is fairly common today to read of professional athletes refusing to sign contracts with their teams until they are given higher salaries. These demands, which can be for hundreds of thousands of dollars, are regarded by team owners as a form of blackmail. The players, however, believe that their skills are a saleable commodity and that they are justified in getting as high a salary as they can bargain for. Are such demands justifiable? Are they only so in certain circumstances? Explain.

6 In the early days of the labor union movement, workers were often treated unfairly. Working hours and conditions were injurious to their health, wages were unfairly low, and fringe benefits were nonexistent. Today the situation is different. Some unions have achieved most of their reasonable demands. But because of the pressure to keep winning new benefits, they make ever more extravagant demands, and use the threat of strikes to gain them. Do union demands ever become an unethical use of power? If so, in what circumstances?

7 Strip mining is the digging of shallow deposits of coal. It has been shown to ruin the land for all agricultural use. Recent experiments in reclaiming stripmined land (for example, by dumping sewage on it) have shown signs of promise. But there is still no certain reclaiming technique. Is strip mining ethical?

8 Investment brokers sometimes have a few clients who live hundreds of miles from their offices. For example, a Wall Street broker may provide investment counseling for his hometown relatives in upstate New York. By arranging to see them during his vacation visits home, he can claim his plane fare or car rental fees and perhaps even many of his meals as business expenses. In other words, he can deduct them on his income tax return and, if he is employed by a company, claim them on his expense account. Is this practice ethical?

9 In some businesses—for example, advertising—executives are quite mobile, changing jobs with unusual frequency. An executive planning such a change can increase his worth to his new employer by taking his clients with him; that is, by meeting with them before he leaves the company and encouraging them to switch their business to his new employer. Discuss the ethical considerations of this practice.

10 Certain hotels do a good share of their business in "hot bed" rentals —the rental of rooms by the hour for purposes of prostitution. They do not employ the prostitutes nor do they have any direct connection with their trade. They merely allow them to check into a hotel room 10 or 15 times a night, each time with a different partner. Is it moral for hotels to permit this use of their premises? Is it moral for a hotel clerk to work in a hotel in which this practice is allowed?

11 Restauranteurs may be strongly tempted to increase their profits by buying old, chemically preserved meat at discount prices or by reheating the same food several days in a row. Discuss the morality of such practices.

12 Heavy construction companies must usually engage in competitive bidding for their contracts. This practice demands that they anticipate every material and labor cost months and even years ahead and commit themselves to complete a project for a specified amount of money. A mistake in calculating or a failure to anticipate a significant increase in prices can bankrupt a company. Is it ever ethical for a construction company to use materials that are slightly substandard in order to offset such errors or increased expenses and thereby remain solvent?

13 An employee's worth to his employer may diminish well before he is eligible for retirement. Many an employer is faced with the dilemma of choosing between retaining an old and trusted yet unproductive worker for 5 or 10 more years, or firing him and jeopardizing his retirement. Does an employer have a moral obligation to such employees? In discussing this, be sure to mention any special circumstances that would alter your judgment.

14 With the costs of running a business increasing every year, efficiency is more and more the byword of the successful businessman. And the axioms of the efficiency expert are "Eliminate what need not be done; simplify what must be done; combine tasks wherever possible." Putting these axioms into practice means, of course, eliminating people's jobs. Under what circumstances is it moral to do so?

15 Book publishers are always in search of a bestseller. And when they find a manuscript that they feel has the requisite qualities for success, they try to offer the author the most attractive contractual terms they can to induce him to sign with their company. Sometimes they will realize that a competitor is in a better position to market the book than they are, and that the author would therefore do better to sign with the competitor. Is it ethical for them to withhold that information from the author?

16 Living in a neighborhood where a house of prostitution flourishes understandably upsets many people, especially those with children. In cases where the house is rented, a group of citizens may band together and pressure the landlord to evict the prostitutes. Is it morally acceptable for them to do this?

Medicine

1   Some medical clinics participate in the testing of drugs that are still in the experimental stage. In such situations the Food and Drug Administration stipulates that the physician must explain to the patient the nature of the drug, its possible benefits, and the element of risk in using it. In certain situations, however, a physician may decide not to provide those explanations. The number of his patients may be so large that he feels he cannot spare the time to do so, or his patients may be generally uneducated and therefore likely to be confused by details. Does either of these reasons justify a physician's withholding explanation? Can you think of any other reason that would?

2   Is it ever morally justifiable to use orphans for medical research? For example, would it be justifiable to catheterize the urinary tracts of infants in an orphanage for a study of bacteria present in healthy individuals? (Such an experiment would pose no danger to the infants.)

3   Though outlawed in some states, the practice of fee-splitting is widespread in medicine. It consists of a physician, usually a general practitioner, referring patients to a particular surgeon, and the surgeon in turn sharing part of his fee with the referring physician. Is this practice ethically acceptable?

4 Some hospitals are publicly financed and controlled. Others are run by private individuals or corporations and operated on a profit-making basis. The latter, by their nature, are run like a business, with an emphasis on efficiency and a profit margin calculated in the charges for room, medication, and surgical costs. Is it ethical for hospitals to be profit-making?

5 In some cases expensive medical treatments are necessary to maintain life, yet are out of the average person's financial reach. An example is the artificial kidney. To pay for such treatment a person must wipe out his savings and even mortgage his house and valuables. To qualify for state aid, he must in effect be prepared to take a pauper's oath. Such a situation is obviously tragic. Is it also unethical in any way? Explain.

6 The choice of who should be given priority in the use of a rare and expensive machine like the artificial kidney can be an agonizing one. Very often it is a life or death decision for the many patients whose existence depends on it. Make a list of the most important considerations that should be made in reaching such a decision and comment on the relative importance of each.

7 Some countries, notably Great Britain, have initiated maintenance programs for drug addicts. Merely by signing up, an addict becomes entitled to free drugs in doses sufficient to stabilize and maintain his habit. Such programs reduce the incidence of drug-related crimes and facilitate research into the phenomenon of addiction. Some critics, however, claim that these programs are immoral because they approve and support physically and emotionally harmful behavior. Is this criticism ethically valid?

8 Members of the Jehovah's Witness religious sect believe that blood transfusion is sinful. If they or their children suffer a serious accident and lose enough blood to require transfusion, they must in conscience refuse it. This poses a dilemma for attending physicians. Consider the following cases and decide whether the physician should or should not administer the transfusion. (In each case, the patient is not likely to survive without transfusion.) (a) The patient is an adult and, while conscious, demands he not receive blood. (b) The patient is an adult, but is unconscious; his wife states that were he conscious he would not accept blood. (c) The patient is a child; he is unconscious; his parents refuse to sign the permission form.

9 For a long time in Western civilization, autopsy was regarded as an immoral practice that profaned the dead person. As a result of this view, there was no legal way for medical school professors and students to obtain corpses. Dedicated to their art, frequently they either dug up recently buried corpses or paid others to do so, without the consent of the dead person's relatives. Were it not for this ghoulish practice, medical science would surely not have developed nearly so extensively or rapidly as it has. Was the practice ethically justifiable?

10 Psychologists and psychiatrists often deal with cases of impotence. As part of their treatment of unmarried patients, they may prescribe a visit to a prostitute. This practice is illegal, of course. Is it also immoral?

11 About one baby out of every six hundred born in the United States is mongoloid. Such children have slanted eyes, broad noses, and I.Q.s of about 30. Many are born with fatal physical defects: parts of vital organs may be missing, the intestines may be blocked, or the heart may not function properly. Often surgery is necessary if they are to survive beyond the first few days of life. The parents must face the question of whether to permit such surgery and save the child, which would mean spending thousands of dollars for special care and education (and in some cases, for institutionalization); or whether to withhold permission and let the child die. Anthony Shaw, an associate professor of surgery and pediatrics at the University of Virginia Medical Center, cites the conflicting views of surgeons over the morality of withholding permission.[1] One is that in any such situation, not operating would be tantamount to murder. Another is that operating would be wrong because "the emotional and financial costs involved are too great to justify the procedure." The third, Shaw's own, is more flexible. He believes that the circumstances, which can be fully evaluated only by the parents, may make operation right in one case, but wrong in another. Which position is most ethically sound and why?

12   Serious accidents can leave their victims comatose for months and even years. The longer the coma lasts, the less chance the person has of regaining consciousness. There are people who live in that state, cared for at considerable expense in hospitals or nursing homes, unable to relate to their loved ones, unaware that they are technically alive. Such cases inevitably raise the question of euthanasia (mercy killing). Merely by injecting a poisonous substance into a vein, a doctor or nurse could spare the victim his limbo of near-life and grant him a painless death. Would it be ethically justifiable to do so in such a situation? Would it be justifiable in any other situation?

13   The development of organ transplant techniques has increased the need for donors. And since such organs as the heart can only be (ethically) removed from persons who have just died, the age-old question "when does death occur?" has taken on new importance. Some medical authorities say it occurs when the heart has stopped beating and fails to respond to massage or chemical stimulants. Others say when the central nervous system has ceased to function (that is, when reflexes cannot be aroused). One authority, Hans Jonas, however, reasons as follows: *"Since we do not know the exact border-line between life and death,* nothing less than the maximum definition of death will do—brain death plus heart death plus any other indication that may be pertinent—before final violence [for example, the taking of an organ for transplant purposes] is allowed to be done."[2] Keeping in mind that Jonas' conclusion would reduce the number of transplant donors, evaluate his reasoning in light of the principles in this book.

14   The same medicine purchased under the generic name costs considerably less than when purchased under a brand name. Yet doctors often prescribe by brand name. Is it ethical for them to do so?

15 According to at least one authority, a number of doctors around the country are prescribing amphetamines rather freely for their patients. Is this practice ethical? In answering, consider that amphetamines are habit-forming and can produce symptoms of schizophrenia and paranoia.[3]

Science

1   In Tennessee the site of an old Cherokee Indian village will soon be flooded in the process of creating a new Tennessee Valley Authority dam. In an effort to find and preserve the artifacts of Indian civilization known to be buried in the area, archaeologists from a University of Tennessee museum have undertaken extensive digging. The Cherokee Indians object to the dam because it represents "flooding a whole race of people's history and heritage off the map." They also object to the digging, which in their view desecrates the graves of their ancestors.[1] Evaluate the morality both of the government's building the dam and of the archaeological team's digging the area.

2   Several years ago a study was made to determine the psychological effects of oral contraceptives. About four hundred poor women participated, most of them Mexican-Americans with large families, who had sought family planning assistance. Some of the women were given oral contraceptives; others were given dummy pills with no birth control chemical. As a result, six of the women in the "dummy group" became pregnant.[2] Evaluate the ethical character of the study.

3   It is now possible for a woman whose husband is sterile to be artificially inseminated with the semen of a donor. Is this practice ethical? If it is in

some circumstances but not in others, be sure to explain those circumstances carefully.

4   It will someday be possible for a woman whose ovaries cannot produce an ovum to "borrow" one from a donor. Would this practice be ethical? If so, under what conditions?

5   The time is 1980. A businesswoman wants to have a baby but can't spare the nine months. So she goes to a laboratory and, following a new scientific technique, "conceives" a baby from her ovum and her husband's sperm. Then she has the fertilized egg implanted in another woman's uterus. Nine months later, the baby safely delivered, she pays the woman for her "labor." Comment on the morality of this procedure.

6   Much of what we hear about the advent of test tube babies still has the ring of science fiction to it. Yet in all probability a successful technique for conceiving and nurturing a human fetus in an artificial uterus is certain to be developed. Naturally such an achievement will be preceded by many fumbling, partially successful efforts. Many scientists, in other words, will be creating human embryos, sustaining them for a time—for a few days at first, and then as their techniques become refined, for a few weeks, three months, seven months. Most, perhaps all, of these embryos and fetuses will be destroyed when they have served their scientific purpose. Is such creation of fetuses ethical? Is their destruction ethical?

7   A scientific organization wishes to conduct research on the effects of ultrasound on human beings. It secures the permission of a local hospital to bombard fetuses that are about to be legally aborted and then to autopsy them after abortion. Is such an experiment ethical?

8   A famous experiment by Yale University's Dr. Jose Delgado dramatized the effectiveness of electrical stimulation of the brain (ESB) as a means of controlling behavior. He "wired" the brain of a fighting bull and demonstrated that merely by pushing a button and sending an electrical current coursing

into the animal's brain, he could stop it in the middle of an enraged charge. He also showed that repeated stimulation diminished the bull's natural aggressiveness. Similar experiments have shown that the same effects occur on humans. For example, a person given to uncontrollable fits of rage can have his brain so wired that, when he feels a seizure coming on, he need only press a button to be instantly calmed. Is the wiring operation ethical if the patient consents to it? Are there any circumstances in which it would be ethical even if he does not consent?

9   Another area of research that shows potential for control of behavior is chemical stimulation of the brain (CSB). Tiny tubes can be placed in strategic parts of the brain and chemicals secreted on timed-release. A given emotional state can thus be maintained in the patient independent of his control. Following are some of the uses CSB might be put to. Examine the morality of each:

(a)   Candidates for high public office (the Presidency, Vice-Presidency, and congress) or for appointive positions such as the President's cabinet could be required to submit to CSB so that the public could be assured no conscious or subconscious aggressiveness in its officials would lead us into war.

(b)   Persons convicted of violent crimes could be treated to assure that they would not act violently again.

(c)   Students who have very short attention spans that hamper their learning or negative attitudes toward teachers and the learning process could be treated to increase their learning potential.

(d)   Every newborn child could be so treated that he would not be susceptible to propaganda or to the promptings of fanatics.

10   In many countries throughout history it has been the practice to use convicts in scientific experiments. The practice continues today. If, for example, a researcher has developed a chemical which preliminary exploratory work indicates will cure a fatal disease, he may seek volunteers from prison populations, administer the chemical to them, and determine its effects on the human body. Or a psychologist studying the effects of extreme variations in climate on the human body may subject consenting prisoners to such variations and test their reactions. Though such experiments are usually very carefully designed to minimize the risk to participants, an element of risk always remains. The participants may become ill or even die of unexpected physical or emotional effects. Because of this danger, volunteers are usually promised special privileges during the course of the experiment and even a reduction of their prison sentences. In cases involving unusual risk, full pardons may be promised. Is it ethical to use prisoners for such experiments? Is it ethical to provide such inducements to volunteers?

11 Sometimes medical school professors encourage their students to volunteer for research experiments. (Student volunteers are used just as prisoner volunteers are, though without rewards; except, of course, the emotional satisfaction of having contributed to progress.) Is such encouragement ethically permissible?

12 Some geneticists, notably Dr. Herman J. Muller, a Nobel Prize winner, have proposed the establishment of banks of stored sperm cells from carefully selected men whose lives had shown unusual mental, emotional, or physical gifts. Couples would then be able to select the genetic material of their choice and therefore produce a child endowed with the heredity that matched their ideals. Evaluate the morality of this proposal.

13 The transplants of such organs as the heart and the kidneys have been shown to be possible. Before too long, scientists assure us, the transplant of the brain will also be a reality. Will such an operation ever be ethically justifiable? In answering, be sure to consider the various activities of the brain and their influence on personal identity.

14 "Cloning" is making carbon copies of individual organisms, genetically exact duplicates. It was first developed in the early 1960s by a Cornell

162

University professor, F. C. Steward, who agitated carrot root cells, causing them to divide and multiply. Eventually he was able to prompt a single cell to develop into a fully-grown carrot plant. Later, Professor John Gordon of Oxford University achieved similar results with a frog. The possibilities of using this technique with animals—for example, beef cattle—and with humans are very real. There are of course technical difficulties that must be solved. But no knowledgeable person doubts that these will eventually be solved. When this happens it will be possible to scrape a cell from a person's hand and create an exact copy of that person, a flesh and blood replica with the same genetic traits. (The procedure would be to destroy the nucleus of an egg cell from a donor and insert in its place the nucleus of any cell of the person to be copied. After being nutured in a nutrient medium for several days, the egg would then be implanted in the uterine wall of the mother.) Thus there could be an unlimited supply of Joe Namaths, Racquel Welches, Kareem Jabbars, Richard Nixons. Since heredity is only part of the influence on a person, their behavior and interests would not necessarily be the same. But their appearance and basic capacities would be. Discuss the morality of cloning.

15   Hans Jonas has suggested that in considering the ethical character of scientific experiments we should distinguish between "averting a disaster" and "prompting a good."[3] In the first, where the goal is *saving* society, Jonas concedes that extraordinary means may be used. But in the latter, where the goal, *improving* society, is less urgent, such means may not be tolerated. "Our descendents have a right to be left an unplundered planet," he reasons. But "they do not have a right to miracle cures. We have sinned against them if by our doing we have destroyed their inheritance—which we are doing at full blast; we have not sinned against them if by the time they come around arthritis has not yet been conquered (unless by sheer neglect). And generally, in the matter of progress, as humanity had no claim on a Newton, a Michelangelo, or a St. Francis to appear, and no right to the blessings of their unscheduled deeds, so progress, with all our methodical labor for it, cannot be budgeted in advance and its fruits received as a due. Its coming-about

at all and its turning out for good (of which we can never be sure) must rather be regarded as something akin to grace." Would Jonas' distinctions be helpful in evaluating any of the preceeding cases (1-14) in this section? Explain.

16 David D. Rutstein made the following assertions about the selection and design of scientific experiments. Do you agree with these assertions? Do they have special application to any of the preceding cases (1-14)? Explain.

(**a**) ". . . In selecting a question for human experimentation, the expectation of benefit to the subject and to mankind must clearly far exceed the risk to the human subject."[4]

(**b**) "It may be accepted as a maxim that a poorly or improperly designed study involving human subjects—one that could not possibly yield scientific facts (that is, reproducible observations) relevant to the question under study—is by definition unethical. . . . Any risk to the patient, however small, cannot be justified. In essence, the scientific validity of a study on human beings is in itself an ethical principle."[5]

War

1 A growing number of people today believe that war is always wrong, that no circumstances ever justify one nation's taking up arms against another. Is the view ethically sound? In answering be sure to comment on the questions of a country's defending itself against aggression and of a strong country coming to the aid of a weak country that has been attacked unjustly.

2 A soldier's thinking about war may change during his service. For example, after experiencing his first real battle and seeing human beings lying dead or in the agony of pain, an enlisted man might be prompted to embrace pacifism and request discharge or transfer to a noncombat unit. Such a request would not be looked on favorably by his superiors and would usually be denied. Since the man had accepted training as a combat soldier, they would reason, he would be obligated to finish his term of service. Is this reasoning morally sound? Would it be morally acceptable for the soldier to continue fighting, even though he objected to it on principle?

3 A career officer may not object to war in general, but may after much observation and evaluation, conclude that his country's involvement in the particular war of the moment is morally unjustifiable. Would any circumstances make it morally acceptable for him to continue to serve in that war? Explain.

4   In the United States, Congress alone has the power to declare or end a war. The President, as Commander-in-Chief of the armed forces, therefore has the legal obligation to keep them informed of his dealings with foreign powers, particularly during wartime. Are there any circumstances in which it would be ethically justifiable for him to conduct secret talks with the enemy and with interested third parties in order to set up the conditions for peace? Would any circumstances justify his lying to Congress? Explain.

5   Over the centuries the experience of war has produced many "conventions," humane rules to limit the devastation and suffering that conflict brings. One of the foremost of these rules is that only military targets will be attacked: that civilian population centers that contain no significant deposit of war supplies and machinery will be spared. Yet during World War II the United States firebombed the German city of Dresden, dropping thousands of tons of TNT and killing more than 100,000 noncombatants. That target was allegedly selected precisely because it was a civilian target and its elimination would demoralize the enemy, and as a result, shorten the war. Discuss the morality of the bombing of Dresden.

6   The dropping of the atomic bomb on the Japanese cities of Hiroshima and Nagasaki was approved because it would make a land invasion of Japan unnecessary and prevent the loss of tens of thousands of American troops. (A land invasion would have destroyed numerous Japanese towns and taken countless Japanese lives, as well.) Yet the atomic bombings leveled two cities, killed well over 100,000, and caused the agony of radiation burns to thousands of people, and genetic damage to their offspring. Discuss the morality of dropping the atomic bombs.

7   Guerrilla warfare consists of terrorization tactics designed to demoralize the enemy and thereby achieve his defeat. Through threats of harm to themselves and their loved ones, civilians are coerced to harbor guerrillas in their villages and to aid them in acts of sabotage. Is it ever ethically justifiable to conduct guerrilla warfare? If so, in what situations?

8   In the summer of 1972, reports from North Vietnam claimed that the United States was engaging in the deliberate bombing of the 2,500-mile network of dikes that protect countless farms and villages from the flooding of the Red River. The U.S. government denied the charges, explaining that any such bombings that may have occurred were accidental. Were such bombing done deliberately, it would have had several obvious consequences. It would have threatened the food supply, the homes and factories, and the lives of tens of thousands of civilians. It would also have hindered the North Vietnamese war effort, prompted them to be less demanding at the conference table, and perhaps hastened the end of the war. Would it have been a morally acceptable policy?

9   The argument that has underlain many of the wartime atrocities men have perpetrated is "they started the war, so we're justified in using whatever means are necessary to finish it." A variation of this which is used whenever it is not clear who "started it" is "they violated the human convention first so we have a right to also." It was used in the Indian wars (though objective scholarship has shown that much of the savagery that was attributed to the Indians was done first by white men). It was used during the First and Second World Wars. It was used in Korea and Vietnam. Evaluate the argument from an ethical standpoint.

10   The practice of torturing prisoners to obtain military information is as old as the art of war. Captives are beaten, subjected to electric shock, made to go without sleep for days, and given little or no food. Is such treatment ever justifiable? Be sure to consider unusual situations as well as more common ones; for example, the situation in which the captive is a guerrilla who, there is reason to believe, may have poisoned a city's water supply or placed a time bomb in a public area.

11   Anticipating the possibility that their soldiers may one day be captured by the enemy, some modern armies include in their basic training exposure to torture techniques. That is, they subject their own troops to mild forms of torture in order that they may learn how to resist torture. Is this practice justifiable morally? If you believe it is justifiable only under certain conditions, specify the conditions.

12 Like every aspect of modern existence, the waging of war is largely technological. Among the weapons now available are bombs that seek out groups of people (presumably the enemy) through heat sensors, and fragmentation bombs that burrow into the earth to await detonation when someone (presumably an enemy soldier) steps on them. Are such weapons morally legitimate in war? Explain.

13 For the fiscal year 1972, the Pentagon set aside approximately ninety million dollars for research into "electro-optical warfare." The device which will be the subject of much of this research is the versatile laser beam. It has the potential for use as an ICBM interceptor. Traveling at the speed of light, it can catch and explode the most sophisticated missiles an enemy might launch. It can ignite wooden targets miles away and can instantly burn out the eyes of anyone who looks directly into it. When aimed at an enemy soldier, it can unerringly burn a fatal hole in his body.[1] Is research into the uses of such weapons ethically justifiable? Is the use of such weapons any less moral than the use of guns?

14 If such weapons as discussed in the preceding question become a reality, would it be morally wrong to work in a company that makes them? To hold stock in such a company?

15 Another avenue of potential for warfare is meteorology. Scientists agree we presently have or will soon have the technological ability to change the earth's temperature, cause tidal waves, create "holes" in the atmosphere that would permit harmful solar radiation to shower selected geographical areas, and create precipitation where we wish. (There have been reports that the latter potential was actually realized by the U.S. in the Vietnam War to impede travel along the Ho Chi Minh trail.) Comment on such practices from an ethical standpoint.

16 A number of Vietnam war protestors, including such well-known figures as the Berrigan brothers, went to prison for their anti-war actions. Was it right for the government to imprison them? Should your judgment of the moral rightness or wrongness of the U.S. involvement in the war affect your answer to this question?

Law

1 In many colleges across the nation, students are required to pay an activity fee that supports cultural, entertainment, and sports programs. Apparently in most cases the student bodies of the colleges originally approved of the idea, and from all indications the majority of students do not object to paying the fee, since the student government decided how the funds are to be used. However, in at least one state, legislators have challenged the idea. Presumably acting on behalf of the minority of students who oppose the fee, a group of New York state legislators introduced a bill several years ago that would forbid any college in the State University system from charging a student activity fee. (The bill was defeated.) Is it ethical for a university to require students to pay such a fee? Does a legislature have the moral right to forbid a university from doing so?

2 Some states still have laws on the books that make fornication, sodomy, and even the practice of contraception by married couples a crime. These laws are seldom applied and the climate of opinion today would surely support their repeal. Yet when they were written it was taken for granted that the state had the moral right, and even the obligation, to make laws about such matters. Evaluate that view, using the appropriate ethical principles from the first twelve chapters.

3 Laws concerning statutory rape are not only still in existence—they are often still applied. (Statutory rape, unlike rape, need not involve the element of force. Any act of intercourse between a minor and an adult is a statutory offense because a minor is held to be incapable of giving consent. The definition of minor, of course, varies from state to state.) Are such laws ethically sound?

4 In the summer of 1972, a young secretary removed her bathing suit on a public beach in New York State. A crowd gathered around her, some to take pictures, others to scold her angrily. Then someone called the police. They arrested her and charged her with "public lewdness." The young woman believes the law violates her rights.[1] Do you agree? Is a law that in effect forces people to wear clothes in public unethical?

5 The job of the police is to protect the health, safety, and welfare of the general public. To meet this responsibility they must obviously not only prevent any activity that threatens the public, but also anticipate such activity before it actually threatens. Many police officials believe that this latter responsibility is moral justification for maintaining close surveillance on political action groups and for dispersing large groups of people listening to inflammatory political speeches. Others disagree, claiming that this line of reasoning leads to the denial of the constitutional rights of free speech and free assembly and to the establishment of a police state. Which position is more in keeping with the ethical principles developed in the earlier part of this book? Explain.

6 Prostitution is illegal in most parts of the United States. Yet, unlike other crimes, it has no victim. Two people freely choose to have sexual contact and to treat that contact as a business transaction. Is it ethical for society to legislate against a victimless act? ("Victim" is of course used here in the legal sense. In a different sense, the emotional and perhaps the moral, it could of course be argued that both participants are victims.)

7 Several years ago the New York City police were accused of using "entrapment" to arrest men who do business with prostitutes. Allegedly, several attractive policewomen in plain clothes were assigned to walk up and down streets where prostitutes were known to congregate. When an unsuspecting man approached one of the policewomen and propositioned her, he was arrested and charged with patronizing a prostitute. Is this technique of apprehending lawbreakers ethical?

8   Is it ever morally permissible for the state to take children away from their natural parents and place them in orphanages or with foster parents? In answering, consider situations in which the parents are alcoholics or drug addicts, or neglect or abuse their children.

9   Capital punishment is the taking of a criminal's life in punishment for his crimes. Throughout history it has been supported by most societies, often even for crimes we would consider minor. During this century, however, more and more people in Europe and America have come to regard it as morally intolerable, even in the case of heinous crimes. Do you agree? Explain.

10   Due to the increase in crime and the inability of the courts to process cases, a practice known as plea bargaining has developed in large metropolitan areas. It consists of the defense attorney making a deal with the prosecution—if the prosecution agrees to reduce the charge against the defendant, the defendant will plead guilty and waive his right to a jury trial. Plea bargaining is appealing to criminals because it allows them to be tried for a lesser crime than they committed. It is appealing to prosecutors because it spares them keeping track of witnesses for months and even years, and to judges because it expedites their handling of cases. Evaluate the morality of plea bargaining.

11   In civil lawsuits it is an established practice for attorneys to charge not flat fees but "contingent fees"—in other words, to have their clients agree in advance to pay them a percentage of their settlement award. In many cases these fees are as high as fifty percent. Evaluate the morality of contingency fees.

12   Is it ethical for attorneys to base their fees on their clients' ability to pay; that is, to charge a rich man much more than a poor man for the same services? Explain your position.

13   The ideal of justice demands that every person charged with a crime receive equal legal representation regardless of race, creed, nationality, or financial status. However, in practice minority groups and the poor receive second-class representation at best. Does the legal profession have any moral obligation to strive to realize the ideal? If so, in what ways might they honor that obligation?

14   There is a controversy today over what kinds of conditions society ought to provide in prisons. Advocates of improved conditions suggest that society has been vengeful in its practices, seeking more to punish than to rehabilitate. They call for more humane conditions, conditions consistent with the human dignity of the inmates. On the other hand, many criticize this liberal thinking as too permissive. Prison should be a drab, monotonous, unpleasant experience, they reason, or it will not deter criminals from repeating their crimes. Discuss the ethical considerations that must be faced in any full discussion of prison conditions.

15   The most controversial moral issue of our time may well be the issue of abortion. The Supreme Court's liberal ruling has not diminished the vigor of debate. The very mention of the issue can trigger emotional outbursts. Most people tend to gravitate toward polar attitudes: "Anything less than abortion on demand is a denial of the most basic right of women," or "Any form of abortion at any stage of pregnancy is premeditated murder." In taking such positions they close their minds to the complexities of the issue and miss the many distinctions that must be made. Any meaningful discussion of abortion must address itself to at least these fundamental questions: Does a woman have absolute rights over her body or are there limitations on those rights? When does life begin? At what stage of prenatal development, if any, is the fetus properly regarded as a person? (This question is a crucial one in the law, since at the moment a person is present the issue of civil rights arises.) Are there sufficient differences among the various kinds of abortion cases to call for different moral judgments? For example, is the case of the fourteen year old victim of rape different from the wealthy, childless society matron? Are either of those cases different from that of the poor woman who already has ten children, or from that of the young married working woman? Discuss the morality of abortion.

Notes

CHAPTER 1

[1] This case was reported in *Time*, June 26, 1972, pp. 74-75.
[2] Andrew H. Malcolm, "Cemeteries Opening Gates for Recreation," *New York Times*, December 10, 1972, p. 1.

CHAPTER 2

[1] Clyde Kluckhohn, *Mirror for Man* (New York: McGraw-Hill Book Co., 1949), pp. 18-19.
[2] May and Abraham Edel, *Anthropology and Ethics* (Springfield, Ill.: Charles C. Thomas Publishers, 1959), pp. 88-89.
[3] Ruth Benedict, *Patterns of Culture* (Cambridge, Mass.: The Riverside Press; and New York: The Houghton Mifflin Co., 1934), pp. 45-46.
[4] *Patterns of Culture*, pp. 210, 216.
[5] *Patterns of Culture*, Chapter 5, "Dobu."
[6] *Mirror for Man*, p. 41.
[7] *Mirror for Man*, pp. 177-78.
[8] *Patterns of Culture*, p. 172.
[9] *Anthropology and Ethics*, pp. 88-89.

CHAPTER 3

[1] All three cases are referred to by Louis Lasagna in "Special Subjects in Human Experimentation," *Daedalus*, Winter, 1969, p. 449.

CHAPTER 4

[1] *Facts on File: 1971*, V. XXXI, No. 1588, p. 248.
[2] *Facts on File: 1956*, V. XVI, No. 800, p. 68.
[3] *Facts on File: 1972*, V. XXXII, No. 1642, p. 296.

CHAPTER 5

[1] "White Slavery, 1972," *Time*, June 5, 1972, p. 24.
[2] "Mummy Removed From Public View," *New York Times*, September 10, 1972, p. 42.

CHAPTER 6

[1] T. W. Adorno et al., *The Authoritarian Personality* (New York: Harper & Brothers, 1950), pp. 147-48.
[2] Else Frenkel-Brunswik, "Prejudice in Children," *Psychology in Action*, ed. by Fred McKinney (New York: Macmillan and Co., 1967), pp. 276-90.

CHAPTER 7

[1] For the important distinction between the rightness of the act itself and the force of the obligation, I am indebted to Kurt Baier's "Responsibility and Freedom," *Ethics and Society*, edited by Richard T. DeGeorge (Garden City, N.Y.: Doubleday and Co., 1966), p. 65.
[2] Jack Anderson, "Army Scientists Move Closer to Orwell's 1984," *The Oneonta Star*, August 5, 1972, p. 5.

CHAPTER 8

[1] *The Right and the Good* (Oxford: Clarendon Press, 1930), Chap. 2.
[2] "The AEC and Secrecy," *Time*, August 14, 1972, p. 73.

CHAPTER 9

[1] "Hollow Holiness," *Time*, August 14, 1972, p. 45.
[2] "Hundreds Reply to Pregnancy Cost Ad," *New York Times*, August 13, 1972, p. 67.
[3] "Road to Survival a Gruesome Path," *Oneonta Star*, December 27, 1972, p. 1.

CHAPTER 10

[1] Henry K. Beecher, "Scarce Resources and Medical Advancement," *Daedalus*, Spring, 1969, pp. 280-81.

CHAPTER 11

[1] Remember that, as explained earlier, the idea of *complete* freedom is an illusion. Our genes and our conditioning limit our freedom to some extent. The question considered here is whether that normal degree of freedom is *further limited* in the particular situation.

CHAPTER 12

[1] "Introduction to the Issue 'Ethical Aspects of Experimentation with Human Subjects,' " *Daedalus*, Spring, 1969, p. x.

[2] Goeffrey Edsall, "A Positive Approach to the Problem of Human Experimentation," *Daedalus*, Spring, 1969, pp. 470-71.

[3] "Respect for Persons," *Daedalus*, Spring, 1969, p. 113.

[4] "Pet Cemetery Boom—A Token of Owners' Devotion," *New York Times*, December 31, 1972, p. 15.

CONTEMPORARY ETHICAL CONTROVERSIES

EDUCATION

[1] *New York Times*, November 26, 1972, p. 41.

SEX

[1] "Under the Yum-Yum Tree?" *The Binghamton Press*, December 12, 1972, p. 1.

[2] Boyce Rensberger, "Clinics for Sex Therapy Proliferate Over Nation," *New York Times*, October 29, 1972, p. 1.

[3] *Ibid*, p. 66.

[4] *Ibid*.

[5] "1986: A Space Odyssey to Mars," *Time*, December 11, 1972, p. 47.

[6] *Ibid*.

GOVERNMENT

[1] George Bria, " 'Tens of Thousands' Are Still Enslaved," *Binghamton Press*, October 28, 1972, p. 4.

[2] Walter Sullivan, "The Lady Was 2,000 Years Old," *New York Times*, August 6, 1972, Section 4, p. 9.

BUSINESS

[1] Jack Anderson, "Double Suicide," *Oneonta Star*, November 24, 1972, p. 4.

MEDICINE

[1] " 'Doctor, Do We Have A Choice?' " *New York Times Magazine*, January 30, 1972, p. 24.
[2] "Philosophical Reflections on Human Experimentation," *Daedalus,* Spring, 1969, p. 244.
[3] "Society Speed," *Time,* December 18, 1972, pp. 76-77.

SCIENCE

[1] Rick Scott, "Indians Charge Heritage Plundered, Flooded Out," *Oneonta Star*, October 2, 1972, p. 1.
[2] Jane Brody, "All In the Name of Science," *New York Times*, July 30, 1972, Section 4, p. 6.
[3] "Philosophical Reflections on Human Experimentation," *Daedalus,* Spring, 1969, pp. 229ff.
[4] "The Ethical Design of Human Experiments," *Daedalus,* Spring, 1969, p. 529.
[5] *Ibid*, p. 524.

WAR

[1] "Now, The Death Ray?" *Time*, September 4, 1972, p. 46.

LAW

[1] "Nude Sunning Faces Court Test," *Oneonta Star*, September 30, 1972, p. 1.